Lead Strong is a powerful message that how to build a firm foundation in Chr... ......, ... continue to form spiritually. This book offers practical and biblical ways to carry out our leadership. Pastor Phil Rasmussen has created a wonderful tool for anyone looking to develop their leadership from a godly perspective.

—Roslyn Bender
Ministry student, Northwest University, Kirkland, WA

It always gives credibility to a book when the author lives out what they are writing about. For as long as I have known Phil, he doesn't just talk about character; he models it. He has maintained a life of godly character, which qualifies him to be a positive influence to equip the next generation in their calling and service to Jesus.

—Rev. Doug Clay
General superintendent of the Assemblies of God, Springfield, MO

Phil Rasmussen has captured the essence of the ingredients that make for greatness in a leader. *Lead Strong* is a comprehensive collection of the essential attributes God uses to change souls as well as societies. This wonderful book will be used by God in building a new generation of Joshuas that our world so desperately needs today. *Lead Strong* is a must-read for any avid student called to serve the purposes of God in his or her generation.

—Dr. Wayne Cordeiro
President, New Hope Christian College, Eugene, OR

If you want to get a grasp on how to spiritually lead and develop the next generation, *Lead Strong* is for you. Dr. Phil Rasmussen has given his career to invest in younger generations. As his student, mentee, colleague, and friend, I spent the past decade with a backstage view of Phil's work, ministry, and life. I confidently say that this book is the compelling marriage of academic research and a lifetime of lived ministry. Anyone can offer an untested theory; *Lead Strong* is an insightful reflection on data and practice, which I have watched and experienced Phil faithfully apply for years.

—Christian Dawson
Campus pastor, Northwest University, Kirkland, WA

In a day and time when there is so much value placed on position, platform, and influence, Phil Rasmussen is a living example of what true leadership, commitment, and ministry look like. I've known Phil over a few decades. I've sat under his leadership. I've personally witnessed his consistency and character. He lives what he writes, and

I am so grateful that he is sharing this wisdom, which will not only benefit pastors and those training for ministry but the future of the church.

—Natalie Grant
Gospel recording artist, Nashville, TN

Philip Rasmussen offers a personal, heartfelt account of the core values for effective leadership with godly character and integrity. The biblical principles he shares on these pages are timeless truths that, when put into practice, will help us all become strong, discerning ministry leaders.

—Dr. Kent Ingle
President of Southeastern University, Lakeland, FL
Author, *Framework Leadership* and *9 Disciplines of Enduring Leadership*

Pastor Phil is a constant source of encouragement and perspective for me personally. I know this book will give you the same!

—Judah Smith
Pastor, Churchome, Seattle, WA

The books I read that impact me most profoundly are those written by authors who possess both a head and heart knowledge of the subjects they address. This means the writer has a firm intellectual grip on his or her material and has a demonstrated lifestyle that reveals that the subject flows from a sincere and practiced heart. Phil Rasmussen does both in his appeal to a future generation of Christian leaders. I know this because my personal acquaintance with the author spans nearly forty-five years. I observed Phil grow as a leader, mentor, and teacher as he personally modeled the leadership principles articulated in *Lead Strong: Developing Character for Ministry Leadership*. I am so pleased he has taken time to capture his insights and experience in this volume. Phil has "talked the talk and walked the walk," which is why I invited him to join our pastoral team in his first vocational ministry post nearly three decades ago. The author's godly character, rooted in the very fruit of the Holy Spirit he describes, allowed me to recommend and endorse Phil Rasmussen for every ministry role he has ever occupied. Phil's appeal for a sound biblical foundation for Christian leadership, his professional ministry experience as a mentor to young leaders, and his personal dedication to the leadership principles offered make this book a valuable tool for both experienced mentors and future Christian leaders alike.

—Rev. Les Welk
Ministry Resources International
Former network leader of the Northwest Ministry Network of the Assemblies of God, Seattle, WA

Lead Strong

Developing Character for Ministry Leadership

Philip J. Rasmussen

WESTBOW
P R E S S®
A DIVISION OF THOMAS NELSON
& ZONDERVAN

WestBow Press books may be ordered through booksellers or by contacting:

WestBow Press
A Division of Thomas Nelson & Zondervan
1663 Liberty Drive
Bloomington, IN 47403
www.westbowpress.com
844-714-3454

Interior Image Credit: Philip Rasmussen

ISBN: 978-1-6642-0361-7 (sc)
ISBN: 978-1-6642-0360-0 (hc)
ISBN: 978-1-6642-0362-4 (e)

Library of Congress Control Number: 2020916366

Print information available on the last page.

WestBow Press rev. date: 09/21/2020

I am grateful that my parents followed Jesus with passion, committed to their calling in such a way that it left an indelible imprint on my life. This book is dedicated to my parents but also to my grandparents, all of whom faithfully committed their lives to ministry.

CONTENTS

FOREWORD

FIRST MET PHIL RASMUSSEN WHEN I WAS AT NORTHWEST University (NU) studying to become a youth pastor. Phil and his wife, Brenda, had taken on the role of campus pastors at NU, and with their extensive background in the area of youth ministry and leadership development, I can remember being excited for what this would mean not only for the climate of our spiritual life as a college but also for what I would gain through being around their influence.

If you have ever met Phil, you know this to be true: he loves and believes in people. Passion comes through his words, his body language, and his eyes. I remember what it felt like as a young college student to have Phil look me in the eyes and tell me that he not only believed in me but he also saw great things in my future. Over the years, I was not only a recipient of this type of care and encouragement; I also saw the many hundreds of students Phil passionately developed for ministry leadership.

I can remember different times Phil would address the need for not only ministry skill but, more importantly, the cultivation of character that would sustain the life in ministry leadership. Over the years, Phil would continue to be a voice of encouragement in my life. Throughout the nearly twenty years since I was a student at Northwest University, his commitment to be a voice of encouragement has continued strong. From the years I served as a youth pastor, to an executive pastor, to serving as the network youth director (a role Phil held years before I did), he has continued to be a friend, a mentor, and a voice God has used in my life.

I have watched, both up close and from a distance, the thousands of lives that he and Brenda have shaped and developed to live out the call on their lives. With that said, I can't think of too many people more qualified to write on this vital topic.

Our world needs strong leadership. Many of us have a picture in our minds of what that means and what that could look like. Some of us see strong leadership as being visionary, and I would agree—that is *part* of strong leadership. Others see strong leadership as courageous. Again, I agree that is *part* of strong leadership. But as I now approach twenty years of local church ministry, serving in a variety of roles and places, having a variety of experiences (both good and incredibly painful), I am convinced that what is needed now more than ever is strong leadership that has developed *character*.

I realized quickly that just because one receives a diploma or title doesn't mean that the character necessary to stay the course and serve the church well is automatically imparted. There have been far too many moments where the lack of character needed has left a trail of wreckage in pastoral leadership. Strong and lasting leadership will be required to stand the tests and trials that come from the unique call to ministry leadership. Character counts, and character doesn't just show up in our lives; it is developed and cultivated with intentionality and with the help of the Holy Spirit leading and guiding our lives.

In *Lead Strong: Developing Character for Ministry Leadership*, Phil clearly lays out the need for character, where it is found, and how it can be cultivated in our lives. Drawing from the truths of the fruit that the Holy Spirit develops in the lives of followers of Jesus (see Galatians 5), Phil lays out how leaders can establish the biblical character necessary to sustain the call to pastoral and ministry leadership. Understand this: these characteristics in the life of pastors and leaders are not optional—they are *essential*. The fruit that the Spirit desires to develop in our lives is not something we can move forward without, but we must be willing to embrace the cultivation process.

As Phil draws from the nine characteristics or fruit that the Holy Spirit develops in our lives, he ties each fruit to a specific leadership quality. These qualities don't happen in our lives automatically. Wouldn't it be nice if they just happened in our lives by default? But as we all know, character is developed over time with intentionality. Each of these leadership qualities Phil addresses leads us to understand and experience a "character outcome" our world needs from those who take up the call to pastoral ministry. We can claim to have character, but true character is revealed in the outcomes of our lives and our leadership.

If you are looking to develop your life today, as well as your life for the future, this book is for you. If you recognize that there are still some areas that need refinement, not only in your "leadership skill" but in your "leadership heart," this book is for you. If you realize that character is the only thing that can sustain you for the long haul in the call on your life, this book is for you. If you are determined to not end up as "a statistic" when it comes to life and longevity in ministry, this book is for you.

What you are about to read is both practical and challenging. It is refreshing and transformational. What you will read in the pages ahead is an opportunity to allow God to do *in* you what you can't cultivate in your own strength or self-determination. The Holy Spirit wants to cultivate and develop your character because it matters. It matters for *you*, and it matters for *the people you will lead*.

Understand this: Character isn't a gift we are given. Character is a quality that is cultivated.

Phil says it well when he says, "Character development entails a lifelong pursuit." None of us ever gets to the place that we graduate from grace or from our need of further development of our character. This is a lifelong journey. And the good news is that Jesus journeys with us each step of the way!

Lean into the grace that God has for your life. Trust in His cultivation process.

Lead strong.

Tyler Sollie
Senior pastor, Life Center Church, Tacoma, WA

PREFACE

THIS BOOK WAS BORN FROM A LIFETIME OF MINISTRY WITH students. I served for twelve years as a youth pastor in the mid-1980s, as a denominational youth leader for six years, as a university campus pastor for sixteen years, and I have now served as a university vice president for the past three years. My current position has given me wonderful opportunities to work with amazing pastors of both large and small churches, parents of college students, noteworthy university staff members, talented faculty members, and hundreds of students and alumni.

The university where I serve affirms the priesthood of all believers (1 Pet. 2:5) and disciples its young people in the process of spiritual formation. Ultimately, the school exists for the formal education and spiritual development of individuals. More than 70 percent of students are earning a liberal arts degree and fully embrace the call of God on their lives to make a difference through marketplace ministry. From its inception until now, the university has also dedicated itself to developing vocational ministers. Many students are preparing for vocational ministry using various learning modules including online courses, church-based internships, extension campuses, and traditional on-campus classes. These young leaders are preparing for pastoral ministry, worship and music ministry, children's ministry, youth ministry, and missions.

In the context of helping people prepare for ministry leadership, I have repeatedly observed that many have remarkable potential for a lifetime of service, but they did not receive foundational spiritual formation in their younger years that is vital to shaping biblical character in their lives. This issue, and the impact it will have on the next generation of church leadership, concerns me deeply. The research I have done and the proposed antidotes I offer in this book have emerged out of my experience. I offer it now to current leaders involved in raising up the next generation of new leaders for kingdom endeavors. This book can be used for ministry training sessions, small group studies, or one's individual devotional development. Its purpose is to reveal the role of the Holy Spirit in the life of the believer and to clearly describe the fruit that His presence should bear in one's character.

ACKNOWLEDGMENTS

A s I REFLECT WITH GRATITUDE ON THOSE WHO HELPED ME with this project, I thank God first and foremost. Throughout this process, I felt the refreshing presence of the Holy Spirit breathe new life into me, urging me to press on with writing and research. I often prayed for inspiration, and there were several crucial moments where I received a touch of wisdom that inspired me to delve deeper.

I also extend heartfelt appreciation to my amazing wife, Brenda. Her words of encouragement are life giving to me. When I pause for a moment to think about the number of people she has coached, mentored, and pastored, I see many faces. She loves people for who they are, yet her words propel people to dream of what they could become. So much of what I have written, the stories, and the ministry experience, could not be possible without a partner like her. I am deeply grateful for my children—Kramer and his wife, Kylie, and Kaitlyn and her husband, Jared—who have dedicted their lives to leading people. They have tremendous wisdom and teach me so much about understanding this generation and the current culture. My family is a treasure to me and I am grateful for their inspiration and support.

To my dear friends, fellow pastors, and the community of staff and faculty members I am privileged to serve alongside, thank you for your encouraging words, love, and support. Every person is so important to me!

INTRODUCTION

The Need

NEW LEADERS TODAY HAVE TREMENDOUS POTENTIAL TO BE the next generation of church leaders, but for many, biblical character development was not a foundational part of their formation process growing up. Leaders often establish their leadership habits by imitating role models or implementing input from instructors and mentors, while remaining disconnected from the most well-established source of godly character—the Holy Spirit (John 15).

Many current ministers will retire within the next generation. They will be replaced by young men and women who have had little to no mentoring. It is crucial that these new leaders come to understand that godly character is the foundation of effective ministry leadership and that they be taught how to cooperate with the Holy Spirit to develop such character.

In my present position at a Christian university, I fill an unusual role where I spend half of my time with students and the other half with pastors. When I am with students, I hear powerful stories—both wonderfully encouraging and gut-wrenchingly difficult. These students have the best of intentions and are facing the future with great excitement, but many of them are new converts and/or did not grow up in dedicated Christian homes. Consequently, they have not yet laid the foundation for or acquired the skills to navigate the challenges of vocational ministry, nor are they connected to the collective wisdom of previous generations of tested and qualified ministry leaders.

A conversation with a new leader preparing for vocational pastoral ministry made this reality very apparent to me. This leader grew up in one of the most dangerous, drug-infested, violent inner-city neighborhoods in the country. In his former lifestyle, he was involved in all these things—drugs, gangs, and criminal activity. Despite all these factors, God miraculously changed his life through the ministry of a family who took him into their home and mentored him. While God was certainly at work in his life, I am thankful he was willing to engage in the process of character development. During our conversation, he introduced me to his roommate. I later found out that she was also his girlfriend and they were sharing a one-bedroom apartment together. Although they were excited about their future in ministry, these two new believers and hopeful leaders had not been taught that living together while pursuing a call in ministry leadership is not the best lifestyle choice. It is my hope and prayer that the thoughts I have written, will help ministry leaders from all back grounds to develop a foundation of character that will propel them to lead strong.

When I interact with pastors, our conversations frequently center on church leadership challenges and the difficulty of finding qualified ministerial replacements. As a large percentage of ministers approach retirement, they express grave concerns and challenges with finding qualified ministry leaders to whom they can eventually pass the baton. Though some denominational schools still have a good track record producing well-prepared ministry leaders to place in churches, a shortage of qualified individuals looms on the horizon.

To give a full picture of the current situation, the average student at the university I serve, only studies for two years.

That means that students preparing for ministry only have four semesters to receive formal biblical training and to engage in the next level of their character development. They are often only able to scratch the surface in both areas. Understandably, the focus of most of a future ministry leader's time at university is on biblical and theological training. Character development typically comes from other sources—such as the investment and input of parents, pastors, and mentors both in childhood and the present. Those who did not grow up with a biblical foundation and/or have recently decided to follow Jesus are at a disadvantage regarding character development.

Another factor in the rapidly shrinking pool of qualified ministerial candidates is that, for various reasons, pastors often encourage their own children to attend secular institutions or to pursue non-ministry degrees. This occurs for three significant reasons, all related to the perspective pastors have gained from their ministry vocation. First, vocational ministry requires long hours and a great deal of work. Second, the demands of ministry have often proven unhealthy for pastors and their families. Third, not only are the hours long and unhealthy, but the compensation is poor. For these reasons, pastors often encourage their own children not to follow them into vocational ministry. No one understands ministry like a child who grows up in a ministry home.

Potential leaders often hesitate to pursue ministry as a career for several reasons. First, ministerial education is expensive, and tuition costs are out of reach for many young people. Second, they may not understand the complexities of a ministry career, subsequently not recognizing the need for formal training in this field. Third, they may not have grown up in a healthy home environment and cannot manage their personal lives. Christian universities try to address some of these challenges by working to make college affordable, providing scholarships to ministry students, preparing students academically, and providing counseling for personal growth. These efforts are valuable and important, but they do not address the need for character development in ministry leaders.

Personally, the school I attended helped me prepare for a ministry career, but my initial preparation began long before I reached college. It started with my parents, who ministered both publicly from the pulpit and privately in our home. They modeled Deuteronomy 6:4–9, repeated by Jesus in Matthew 22:37–40, in which God commands parents to pass on biblical truths to their children.

In the Deuteronomy passage, Moses identifies three specific ways for parents to impress God's precepts upon their children. First, talk about them (Deut. 6:7). Preparing the next generation for leadership must begin with winsome communication about the things of God. Often our family dinnertime conversation would include ministry-related subjects. At times, my parents would ask our opinion about a matter, just to make us think deeply and generate a potential solution. Second, exhibit faithfulness and teach others to live with this kind of faithfulness (v. 8). Praying for people in our home and seeing real miracles occur was formative in my faith. I learned to pray kneeling next to my mother, who would often call out to God for our daily family needs. Third, speak and write about faith and emphasize those character qualities that will demonstrate truth. Daily devotions and a yearly conference on character development was a part of our regular family activities. Committing to live out these scriptural principles in the home does not guarantee the outcome, but this is the role parents are called to in their children's lives. Godly character development cannot be left to chance. Someone who did not grow up in a biblically founded environment will likely need to undergo significant character development before becoming an effective pastoral leader.

A Way Forward

This book lays out an approach for establishing biblical character in leaders preparing for ministry. It is structured using the framework of the fruit of the Spirit. Each chapter focuses on one of the nine fruit of the Spirit, delving into biblical truths about the character development produced by each fruit.

Chapters 1–10 provide a clear biblical-theological foundation for understanding the fruit of the Spirit (as described in Galatians 5:22–23), which comprise a leader's character.

> Chapter 1 examines the tension Paul observed in the Galatian church, which led to his message of grace and his visually rich description of life in the Spirit.
>
> Chapters 2–10 examine the nine fruit of the Spirit as found in Galatians 5, exploring the meaning behind each word in the original language and wrestling with the personal and leadership circumstances that each fruit addresses. For example, the discussion about love includes a biblical response to loving people through difficult times. The chapter on joy examines how we can maintain an attitude of joyfulness during challenging circumstances. The chapter on peace addresses how to maintain a peaceful spirit in the face of opposition. The examination of patience highlights God's patient nature toward humanity. The kindness chapter

uncovers the biblical purpose for being kind. The exploration of goodness wrestles with extending goodness toward hateful people. The chapter on faithfulness focuses on stewardship. Gentleness looks at the truly humble character of Christ. The discussion about self-control examines the mind and our need for the Spirit to govern this powerful instrument.

Chapters 11–20 build upon these fruit of the Spirit to establish subsequent Christ-centered, character-based leadership qualities, which are demonstrable as twenty-six outcomes in a godly leader's life.

Chapter 11 investigates the overall nature of character development, including biblical, psychological, and physiological components.

Chapters 12–20 expand on the nine core biblical leadership qualities (fruit of the Spirit) as seen in Galatians 5, connecting them to the twenty-six character outcomes. As leaders develop lives abundant with the fruit of the Spirit, these outcomes become increasingly evident and form the foundation of their godly leadership.

Chapters 21–23 have some final reflections and resources to practically apply the book's content.

Chapter 21 contains a sample character development curriculum, which can be utilized in a seminar, class, or other instructional scenario. This material can also be adapted for a sermon series, small group study, or personal reflection.

Chapter 22 contains a character development survey, which can be used to gather feedback on how the material helped participants engage in their own character development process. Data from this assessment tool can also help determine participants' receptiveness to Spirit-inspired leadership and their understanding of the significant role such leadership should play in their lives. The chapter includes additional evaluation suggestions as well.

Chapter 23 contains final thoughts on the implications of this study.

It is my hope that as leaders develop godly character qualities and dependence on the Holy Spirit through a solid spiritual formation process, they will become rooted and established in their leadership, able to lead the church well into the future.

The Fruit of the Spirit

IRST, LET US FOCUS ON THE CHARACTER DEVELOPMENT principles that are revealed in scripture, primarily the fruit of the Spirit. A spiritual leader who endeavors to represent the true gospel of the New Testament must exhibit this fruit. God's Word calls spiritual leaders to live "above reproach," setting an example for others to follow (1 Tim. 3:2). When the apostle Paul was training Timothy to be a church leader, he outlined various qualities necessary for exemplary leadership. Likewise, in his letter to the Galatian church, he taught that through Jesus's fulfillment of the law, we can receive the promised Holy Spirit and be empowered to gain godly character (Gal. 3:14, 5:5–6).

The book of Galatians voices a relevant message to church leadership today. Legalism, present in Paul's lifetime, also exists in our churches. Paul emphasized faith and grace over legalism. In this book, we will examine the culture of the Galatian church and the tensions between those focused on legalism and those emphasizing the faith and grace of the gospel. This will set us up to learn about the character qualities that the Holy Spirit produces in us as believers and leaders when we abide not in legalism, but in Christ.

CHAPTER 1
Paul's Condition

T o understand Paul's message to the Galatians, it is critical that we understand the context in which he wrote. Paul was a skilled rhetorician and chose his words carefully to establish his position. He used deliberative rhetoric to urge Galatian Christ followers to hold on to his original teachings about the gospel and to disregard the false teachings of those who opposed the gospel message. His persuasive approach conveyed his urgency to correct the Galatians.[1]

Paul started the church in Galatia through the power of the Spirit (Gal. 3:1–5). After his departure, it became infiltrated by false teachers, and a distorted gospel message invaded the church (1:6–7). Thus, Paul accused them of "so quickly deserting" the grace of Christ. Most likely, the recipients were familiar with Paul's turn of phrase. The expression he used was of Syrian origin and was like a saying in 2 Maccabees describing rebellious Hellenistic Jews who turned from their faith during the Maccabean revolt—an event that occurred two centuries before this event in the Galatian church. Paul knew that his audience was primarily Jewish and that this loaded comparison would catch their attention.[2]

Paul continued to use pointed language to indicate his irritation with those who had tampered with the gospel message he had preached. He said, "If anybody is preaching to you a gospel other than what you accepted, let them be under God's curse" (Gal. 1:9). Clearly, Paul felt disturbed by what was happening in the Galatian church, but he cast a wide net to include anyone who had discredited the original gospel message. In using the word *anybody,* he not only refers to the current church leaders who were distorting the truth, but also includes himself or any other apostle who might preach another message besides the gospel of Jesus Christ.[3]

As Paul closed the letter, he emphasized again the urgency of the situation: "See what large letters I use as I write to you with my own hand!" (Gal. 6:11). Customarily, a scribe trained in penmanship would write letters at that time, while the sender dictated the content. Paul felt it so necessary to address this issue that he concluded with a personalized, handwritten note to his "brothers and sisters" (v. 18). He seemed hopeful that his relationship with them would remain intact, though not at the expense of the gospel message he was charged by Christ to proclaim.[4]

The Tension

Paul's concern for the Galatian church caused him to address them with intensity. The people in this church probably knew Paul personally, as he refers to them as brothers and sisters (Gal. 5:11). Nevertheless, he became so disturbed that he confronted them at the possible expense of their close friendship. Conceivably, Paul was distressed by their disrespect for the gospel, their unfaithfulness, their lack of character, and the injustice they were perpetuating. As we become familiar with the original message Paul proclaimed to the Galatians, we can begin to understand his agitated response to their departure from it.

Galatians 2:16 summarizes the true gospel Paul preached: "A person is not justified by the works of the law, but by faith in Jesus Christ. So, we too have put our faith in Jesus Christ that we may be justified by faith in Christ and not by the works of the law, because by the works of the law no one will be justified." Paul proclaimed the good news that believers no longer live under the law but under grace. God no longer required people to perform rituals to attain holiness but rather He accepted them freely through faith in His holy Son.

In his greeting, Paul reestablished his authority and apostleship. As a missionary appointed by the church of Antioch, Paul did not preach a message based on human authority, or even based on the authority of the Antioch church, but rather one based on the authority he had received from God through Jesus Christ (Gal. 1:1).[5] Paul's calling lent weight and credibility to his message.

Up to the point of Jesus's death and resurrection, attaining God's favor required keeping the Mosaic law. In Galatians 3 and 4, Paul points out that the true standard was never whether a person perfectly kept the law. Rather, the basis for justification was always through faith, not through works. Paul holds up the example of Abraham, whom God declared righteous based on his faith long before the establishment of the law.[6] F. F. Bruce substantiates this concept of righteousness by faith:

> God promised [Abraham] that his offspring would be more numerous than the stars he could see in the night sky. Nothing could have seemed less likely, yet Abraham believed this incredible

promise because of the trustworthy-ness of Him who made it: "he believed in Yahweh, and He [Yahweh] reckoned it to him as righteousness" (Gen. 15:6).[7]

Paul's message of grace through faith is as true for us believers today as it was for Abraham and for the Galatian church. God is faithful to His promises—unchanging—and can be trusted when we put our faith in Him.

Paul concluded his correction of the Galatian church by addressing legalistic believers' concerns about those who no longer followed the former laws of righteousness. They argued that without the Torah, people would behave however they thought was right, even if it wasn't. In Galatians 5 and 6, Paul refuted this argument by teaching that the Holy Spirit, who indwells believers, leads them closer to Jesus Christ and instructs them in right relationship with Him. This connection forms a new nature wherein believers' personal desires become more righteous. In short, the Holy Spirit cultivates an internal change that produces godlike fruit (Gal. 5:22–23).[8] There are two essential themes in Paul's message: (1) the work of Christ on the cross is sufficient to make us righteous through faith, and (2) the Holy Spirit empowers us to live a life reflective of the gospel.[9]

The Message

Paul crafted his argument to arrive at an understanding of what it means for the Spirit of Christ to live in believers. He arrived there with a simple yet profound premise: the time of the Torah/law is gone, and a new era governed by the Spirit has arrived.

The first two chapters of Galatians are autobiographical. Paul shares his own testimony and begins to diagnose the situation the Galatian church is experiencing. Chapters 3 and 4 provide doctrinal correction addressing the Galatian churches' drift away from the true gospel. Chapters 5 and 6 conclude the letter with practical application.[10] This chapter focuses on Paul's personal account of his conversion and growth in Christ as it relates to the fruit of the Spirit.

Paul's own relationship with Jesus—"Christ lives in me"—directly informed his understanding of how the Holy Spirit works within believers (Gal. 2:20). Cross-referencing Paul's statement with Romans 8:9–10 helps us to understand him better. In Romans, Paul proclaims that a person is not of Christ if the Spirit of God is not at work in his or her life. Paul outlines a clear dynamic in which the Spirit gives life to believers through Christ's righteousness. As they learn to walk by the Spirit who is at work in their lives, they will "bear the fruit" of (i.e., look more like) the one who gave the Spirit—Jesus.[11] When we fully entrust ourselves to the person of Jesus, the presence of God's Spirit becomes evident in our character. Such character is essential for spiritual leaders to set the example for godly living.

The Source

As Paul moves toward the pragmatic portion of his letter, he intro-duces a metaphor. After listing fifteen behavioral traits of individuals who are not guided by the Spirit (Gal. 5:19–21), Paul uses an image to transition and to introduce that which ought to proceed from someone who does live by the Spirit. Paul employs an agrarian metaphor, which would have resonated with the people to whom he was writing. He begins by saying, "But the fruit of the Spirit is …" (5:22). Jesus also used figurative imagery of fruit several times (Matt. 7:17–18; Luke 6:43–44).[12] In John 15:1, Jesus declares, "I am the true vine, and my Father is the gardener." There are several observable truths in John 15. First, to produce the best quality fruit, one must plant the right vine. Fruit cannot differ from or be better or worse than its parent source. When Jesus says, "I am the vine," He uses the Greek word *alethinos*, which indicates that He is the "true" or "real" vine. Connecting to the true vine is the only way to produce real fruit. Any other source produces counterfeit fruit.[13] Merrill C. Tenney notes the vital role of the real vine: "No fruit can be better than the vine that produces it. Jesus said, 'I am the true vine.' Unless the believer is vitally connected with Him, the quality of his fruitfulness will be unacceptable. There may be many branches, but if they are to bear the right kind of fruit, they must be a part of the real vine."[14] For a person to have maximum kingdom impact, he or she must connect to the real source for his or her life to resemble godly character qualities.

The second truth is that God the Father is the vine keeper. Success in growing fruit depends upon the skill of the one tending the crops. The good vine keeper knows his craft well and understands how to tend, protect, and cultivate the vine to produce the best yield. Christian leaders must entrust themselves and their ministries to God, the vine keeper, to produce healthy spiritual fruit.

Leaders often have difficulty trusting God with the pruning process in their own lives. Jesus says, "[The Father] cuts off every branch in me that bears no fruit, while every branch that does bear fruit He prunes so that it will be even more fruitful" (John 15:2). Leaders can expect two things to happen to them. One is that they will be pruned. The Greek verb *aireo*, which means "to take away," refers to what is done to areas of our lives that are not bearing fruit. In the agricultural world, this involves the vine keeper literally removing dead wood from the vine. The other procedure a leader will go through is that of continual sanctification. Jesus uses the Greek term *kathaireo* to describe this process, which means "to clean or purify." The vine keeper cares about his fruit-bearing vines enough to cleanse and purify them so that they will increase in health and productivity.[15]

Third, John 15 emphasizes the necessity of leaders staying connected to the vine. Jesus says, "Remain in me" (John 14:7). At times, a leader can produce that which appears to be fruit, using only personal skill and charisma. This is a mere synthetic production, rather than the real, life-giving fruit of a true, vital connection with the vine. If leaders want to see good fruit produced throughout a lifetime of faithfulness, they must remain connected to the source, the vine of Jesus. The quality and quantity of fruit will likely be different for every person based on the individual's relationship with the vine keeper. Some will have a deep and intimate growing faith, able to see miracles occur through intercessory prayer. Others may see many come to know and grow in Christ through preaching and teaching.

The fourth observation of this passage is that one who does not bear fruit may not be a true disciple. Bearing fruit is evidence of true discipleship. Jesus said, "This is to my Father's glory, that you bear much fruit, showing yourself to be my disciples" (John 15:8). Jesus identified a real believer as one who bears fruit and represents God—the vine keeper—in an honoring way. This is a teaching that he also addresses in Matthew 7:20 and Luke 6:43–44. Above all, the character, or fruit, in a leader's life should bring glory to God.

My wife loves roses. Over the past few years, I have created a rose garden in the backyard for her enjoyment. I am not an expert rose gardener, but at last count, I had twenty-six rose bushes in the garden. Those twenty-six have come at a cost since I have planted at least ten that have not survived. Learning to be a good gardener takes patience, research, and perseverance, especially with roses.

Roses often have a lot of issues, such as fungus, rust, and bugs. Working with them, I have discovered that the ones with the most beautiful blooms also have the sharpest thorns. In many ways, my rose bushes are like people. I have even named some of them after real people I know. My roses have taught me that God—the good gardener—has great patience with us as we work through issues that are damaging our lives. He wants the best for us, even if that means that sometimes He must prune us to make way for better flowers to grow. When a rose or a branch dies, the gardener must trim the branch, or deadhead it, to make room for new growth. Many times, as I have worked to improve my plants, their sharp thorns have reached out and scratched me and caused me to bleed. I have become thankful that God is a patient gardener who takes His time, cutting away damaged areas of our lives to make room for beautiful character to bloom in its place.

The process of becoming a disciple of Jesus, which is often called Christian spiritual formation, need not be approached with fear but can rather be embraced with enthusiasm. Sometimes when we think about this notion of God pruning and cutting away things in our lives, apprehension arises. The primary quality that should color all the rest of a leader's character is love. Love binds us to Christ, keeping us connected to the vine. Jesus said, "As the Father has loved me, so have I loved you. Now remain in my love. If you keep my commands, you will remain in my love, just as I have kept my Father's commands and remain in His love" (John 14:9). Christian leaders should embrace the pruning process, knowing that our heavenly Father wants the best for His children, and that only legitimate children receive discipline and become true heirs, able to receive their father's inheritance (Heb. 12:7–8, 10).

One of the primary practices that leads to the production of healthy fruit, or Christian character, is the habit of withdrawing to a place of solitude to pray and listen to the Spirit. For most of us, our hurried lives make it difficult to hear the voice of the Spirit. The psalmist implores believers to "wait on the Lord" and quiet themselves as they seek God's presence (Ps. 130:5–6).[16] Jerry Bridges affirms that becoming Christlike requires intentional pursuit:

> Christian character flows out of devotion to God, and it confirms the reality of that devotion in practical ways. We may express a reverence for God, we may lift our hearts in worship to Him, but we demonstrate the genuineness of our devotion to God by our earnest desire and sincere effort to be like Him. Paul not only wanted to know Christ, he wanted to be like Him, and he pressed forward with utmost intensity toward that goal.[17]

Jesus himself exemplified what it means to quiet one's spirit by frequently drawing away to quiet places to pray (Luke 5:16). There are many influences that affect leaders, including full schedules and organizational and societal pressures. Going away to a quiet place is essential to cultivate the ability to hear and know God's voice and to discern His work in the soul.

In the past, I have struggled with making time to quiet my spirit and spend time in solitude with God. My schedule is as full as most people's, and the continued demand for my time never seemed to stop. I realized that I had to be intentional, prioritizing time with God on my calendar. The urgent will always demand time from the important. What is important must be put on the calendar first, or the urgent will take its place. So, I have an immovable daily appointment on my calendar for quiet time with the Lord. Every morning, before my workday starts, I have a calendar entry that says "Prayer." The last thing I look at before I go to bed each night is my schedule for the next day. In that routine moment, I remember that the first appointment I have in the morning is with God. No other meetings can be scheduled during that time; it is booked and nonnegotiable.

Paul does not say that the believer produces many fruits (plural), but rather fruit (singular)—Holy Spirit fruit. The difference between fruits and fruit is that all fruit comes from its own type of tree, not from several types of trees. The Holy Spirit is the only source of spiritual fruit.[18] When people come in contact with a leader who demonstrates character qualities, or fruit, that have been produced by a life lived in the Spirit, they will want to know more about it. They will be intrigued at how that person treats others with kindness, speaks truthfully, remains patient, and endures hardships. Such a person can plant seeds in other people's lives, with the hope that they, too, will develop Spirit-led character as they learn to connect to the vine and begin the process of bearing fruit.

The Advocation

As Paul reestablished the original gospel message given to him by Christ through the Holy Spirit, he points the Galatian believers toward a better way to live. Their freedom in Christ should propel them into a life in the Spirit. As Paul sets up this significant portion of Galatians, he uses the verb "walk" (*peripateo*) (Gal. 5:16). He uses this verb thirty times throughout his writing, but only one time in Galatians.[19] In so doing, he emphasizes the important point that walking in the Spirit is the lifestyle to which believers are called.[20] Paul records nine character qualities that should be in a believer's life as he or she cultivates a resemblance to God the gardener. These are: love, joy, peace, patience, kindness, goodness, faithfulness, gentle-ness, and self-control (v. 22).

In his letter, Paul addressed his friends as brothers and sisters, reminding them that their new freedom in Christ was not intended to entice them toward earthly desires but rather to serve one another in humility and love as the family of God (Gal. 5:13). Paul echoes the greatest commandment, given by Jesus: love one another (Mark 12:31). In loving God and loving their neighbors (all people), Christ followers fulfill this commandment and avoid falling into the trap of fleshly desires that Paul earlier describes.[21]

The fruit of the Spirit that Paul delineates in Galatians 5:22–23 appear throughout the entirety of scripture. These attributes exhibit the very essence of God's nature.[22] Below is a snapshot of scriptural places where the fruit of the Spirit is mentioned:

Aspect	Definition	Attribute of God	Attribute for Christians
Love	Sacrificial, unmerited deeds to help a needy person	Exod. 34:6 John 3:16 Rom. 5:8 1 John 4:8, 16	John 13:34–35 Rom. 12:9, 10 1 Pet. 1:22 1 John 4:7, 11–12, 21
Joy	An inner happiness not dependent on outward circumstances	Ps. 104:31 Isa. 62:5 Luke 15:7, 10	Deut. 12:7, 12, 18 Ps. 64:10 Isa. 25:9 Phil. 4:4 1 Pet. 1:8
Peace	Harmony in all relationships	Isa. 9:6–7 Ezek. 34:25 John 14:27 Heb. 13:20	Isa. 26:3 Rom. 5:1; 12:18; 14:17 Eph. 2:14–17
Patience	Putting up with others, even when one is severely tired	Rom. 9:22 1 Tim. 1:16 1 Pet. 3:20 2 Pet. 3:9, 15	Eph. 4:2 Col. 1:11 Heb. 6:12 James 5:7–8, 10

Kindness	Doing thoughtful deeds for others	Rom. 2:4; 11:22 Eph. 2:7 Titus 3:4	1 Cor. 13:4 Eph. 4:32 Col. 3:12
Goodness	Showing generosity to others	Neh. 9:25, 35 Ps. 31:19 Mark 10:18	Rom. 15:14 Eph. 5:9 2 Thess. 1:11
Faithfulness	Trustworthiness and reliability	Ps. 33:4 1 Cor. 1:9; 10–13 Heb. 10:23 1 John 1:9	Luke 16:10–12 2 Thess. 1:4 2 Tim. 4:7 Titus 2:10
Gentleness	Meekness and humility	Zech. 9:9 Matt. 11:29	Isa. 66:2 Matt. 5:5 Eph. 4:2 Col. 3:12
Self-control	Victory over sinful desires		Prov. 16:32 Titus 1:8; 2:12 1 Pet. 5:8–9 2 Pet. 1:6

The following chapters explore each fruit of the Spirit that God desires believers, and thereby ministry leaders as well, to exhibit.

CHAPTER 2

Love

I T IS NOT SURPRISING THAT LOVE IS FIRST ON THE LIST OF characteristics of the Spirit-filled life. The central message of the Bible is love—beginning with God, who is love (1 John 4:8). Christ embodies this true love, which God bestows upon all believers. Christlike love is called *agape* love; the self-giving, self-sacrificing love that Paul mentions in 1 Corinthians 13:4–8. In this passage, Paul presents fifteen thoughts about what love is. He starts by saying, "Love is patient, love is kind" (1 Cor. 13:4). This verse and other portions of the 1 Corinthians 13 passage bear a remarkable resemblance to the fruit of the Spirit, implying that all other fruit proceed from love.[23]

Love Is Active

The word *love* does not appear as a noun in classical Greek writings, but it does appear multiple times as a verb. Paul intended to convey the active nature of love. Early church historian Josephus supported this perspective by referencing love twenty-four times in his writings and never once using it as a noun. The Greeks had three other names for love: (1) *philia*, which refers to a warm, intimate friendship, (2) *eros*, which refers to physical love between sexes, and (3) *storge*, which refers to the love of family members. Biblical passages referring to God's love always use the verb *agape*, which is the same word Paul uses to describe the kind of love believers should have one to another.[24]

According to 1 John 3:16, genuine love looks like a person laying down his or her life for another. When believers respond to others in Christlike ways, they evidence the fruit of the Spirit of love. Dallas Willard makes this insightful observation: "Love, as Paul and the New Testament presents it, is not action—not even action with a special intention—but a source of action. It is a condition out of which actions of a certain type emerge."[25] Without understanding the intrinsically active nature of biblical love, believers may fail to truly live out Jesus's commands. Jesus said, "Love one another as I have loved you. If you obey my commands, you will remain in my love, just as I have obeyed my Father's commands and remain in His love ... My command is this: Love one another as I have loved you" (John 15:9–10, 12). The truth of a believer's, and therefore also a ministry leader's, character is visible through his or her relationship with God, other Christians, and neighbors (whether Christians or not). As a result of relationship with Christ, leaders should see all their interpersonal relationships through the lens of God's love.

It is not normative to love beyond ourselves without the work of God's Spirit in our hearts. Selfless love comes to fruition through intentionality. Love grows out of a personal encounter with the living God.[26] John provides invaluable insight into the development of love in a person's life. We demonstrate love by doing right and loving people (1 John 3:10–11). We love when we are life-giving people (1 John 3:14). We love when our words and actions are truthful (1 John 3:18). We love when we keep the command of God to love others (1 John 3:23). We love when the love of God is seen in us (1 John 4:12). We love because God loves us (1 John 4:16, 19). We love as we walk in obedience to God (2 John 5). John rejects claims that we can be out of fellowship with God, continue to sin, do the works of the devil, or do harm to others, and still be children of God. Those of God will follow His command to love people. It follows, then, that godly leaders will not only embrace this command but will also model it to their followers.

Love and the Disciples

Jesus spent most of His last three years on earth ministering with twelve individuals. He chose to love them through many difficult circumstances but arguably the most challenging was His choice to love Judas. He knew Judas would betray Him, be disloyal to Him, and trade His friendship for money (Mark 14:10–44; John 6:70–71), but He continued to love him, befriend him, and accept him. Jesus knew what Judas was going to do when the time came, but that knowledge did not change His behavior toward him. Another significant moment where Christ demonstrates love was before He ascended into heaven. Luke records the experience of Jesus taking the disciples away to Bethany (Luke 24:50). He lifted His hands, touched each disciple, and pronounced a blessing upon each one of them.

Love through Difficulty

If Christian leaders are to love people who are hurtful, disagreeable, or make life choices that deviate from God's plan, they must stay connected to the source of love. Paul understood this when he encouraged the believers in Thessalonica: "May the Lord make your love increase and overflow for each other ... May He strengthen your hearts so that you will be blameless and holy in the presence of our God and Father when our Lord Jesus comes with all His holy ones" (1 Thess. 3:12–13). When leaders stay connected to the vine and allow God's love to grow in them, the spiritual strength they have within outweighs the faults committed toward them by other people. They can recognize and live out of the truth that "love covers a multitude of sins" (1 Pet. 4:8) and that "there is no fear in love" (1 John 4:18).

Stephen, a significant leader of the early church and one of the first martyrs, likely influenced Paul's perspective of what real love looks like by providing a poignant illustration of it. Stephen loved people, even to the point of forgiving them for his death. As he died, he asked the Lord not to hold his murderers' act of sin against them (Acts 7:60). Jesus also asked His Father to forgive His executioners because they did not know what they were doing (Luke 23:34). Loving to that degree comes from a place beyond normal human strength; it is a Holy Spirit–given gift.[27]

Not long ago, I received a text from a former student that I had counseled when he was at my university. When I met the student, he had come out of an abusive home, married early, and was on the verge of divorce because his spouse was living a secret life of unfaithfulness. At least three years had passed since his graduation when I received this random text from him, which was a solicitation to a new partner. He had accidentally selected my name, which was still in his contacts. It was clear to me that he was on a downward spiral in his faith. I responded to the text, asking if I could help him, reminding him of better days when he had served God faithfully. After a couple of short responses, he requested that I never reach out or contact him again, including statements that he did not know me anymore or have any recollection of our time together. In my flesh, his response hurt, but I believe the seeds planted through our unexpected interaction will continue to grow into fruit as the Holy Spirit works in his life. This was a reminder to me that loving people in their pain is often very messy. It takes a Holy Spirit–driven love to engage with that pain and to be effective.

In twenty-first century Western culture, love and judgment are often pitted against each other. Scripture teaches believers not to judge another person (Matt. 7:1–2). James instructs believers not to speak evil against one another (James 7:24). Paul says that when passing judgment on another, one condemns oneself (Rom. 2:1). In a world ravaged by sin, Christians often find it difficult to love rather than to judge. Judgment is best left to God, who is authorized to both love and judge based on the holiness of His character. D. A. Carson comments about God's wrath; an element of His judgement:

> Wrath, unlike love, is not one of the intrinsic perfections of God. Rather, it is a function of God's holiness against sin. Where there is no sin, there is no wrath, but there will always be love in God. Where God in His holiness confronts His image-bearers in their rebellion, there must be wrath. Otherwise God is not the jealous God He claims to be, and His holiness is impugned. The price of diluting God's wrath is diminishing God's holiness.[28]

Since the Giver of judgment is also the Giver of love, believers would do well to choose the better of the two options. Since love is the best reflection of who God is, it is prudent to demonstrate love to one another. For Christian leaders, when someone they

19

are leading makes a course correction, leaders should ensure that person feels loved through the process. When a leader discerns the need to provide correction or admonishment to those they lead, they should seek to do so in a manner that reflects the loving heart of God.

CHAPTER 3

Joy

MANY PEOPLE WORK A LIFETIME TO OBTAIN JOY, WHICH IS the second characteristic of life in the Spirit, but few fully embrace it. Believers can only obtain true joy by staying connected to the source of joy, the vine of Christ. Joy comes from a supernatural source. In our natural selves, we struggle to produce this character quality. Paul used the Greek word *chara* to describe joy that is unlike, and so much better than, mere human happiness.[29] Donald Gee expands on this thought:

> There is an entirely natural joy obtainable by entirely natural means. But it is not what is described as a "Fruit of the Spirit." This joy is result of receiving the Spirit and walking in the Spirit. Natural Joy has certain characteristics that sharply distinguish it from spiritual joy ... natural joy does not generally last, and has no elements of permanency.[30]

The Holy Spirit's gift of joy is something entirely different from what the world knows as joy.

Paul encourages believers to "rejoice in the Lord" despite difficult people who do terrible things (Phil. 3:1). This joy comes as you grow in your faith (Phil. 1:25). The unchanging foundation of joy is our faith in God (Rom. 12:12), which originates from the Holy Spirit (14:17). Paul traced the origin of joy to God, which means that it is not dependent upon human emotion but rather upon divine inspiration. Christian joy is not circumstantial; it is a Spirit-inspired gift that can be possessed in the midst of and in spite of circumstances (2 Cor. 6:10; 8:2; 1 Thess. 1:6).[31] James D. G. Dunn substantiates the supernatural source of joy, observing:

> The contrast of joy with the "works of the flesh" is note-worthy: joy by its nature is something uncontrived, often with an unexpected element in it; in this case a consequence of the believer's openness and responsiveness to the leading of the Spirit, affording new experiences of fellowship and new insights into the working out of the gospel.[32]

As Christian leaders follow the guidance of the Holy Spirit and obediently carry out the mission of God, joy is a natural outcome. Temporary joy may be found in the pleasures of the world, but true joy comes from fellowship with the Holy Spirit.

The Apostles

After enduring many unjustified sufferings, the apostles rejoiced because of their belief in Christ (Acts 5:41). They had joy because of the disgrace they experienced for the sake of Christ, who was the perfect example of love. Joy in the face of suffering is counter to today's typical response to unjust persecution. James encouraged those who were suffering to consider their experience pure joy, because testing of faith only increases endurance (James 1:2–3). When Christian leaders find their character wrongfully attacked, they have a choice about how to respond. Knowing that the challenge they are facing will produce stronger character, they can choose joy.

My wife and I have two adult children who are both in full-time ministry. They are a remarkable blessing to us. My son and daughter grew up in a ministry home, where we worked hard to live our faith out in front of them. They both went to public school. Their stories about being committed and vocal Christians in this setting are heartbreaking. In middle school, my son was told by a classmate that if he were to bring a gun to school, my son would be the first person he would shoot. Another time, he was bullied and thrown through a window. In high school, a mob of girls coerced my daughter into a bathroom where they beat her. Later, a young man verbally assaulted her with sexual innuendos. As parents, we did everything possible to protect them, but we could not take away these experiences or their pain. Though these were terrible moments in their lives, my children learned a valuable lesson. Suffering will come, and it is even more likely for those who follow Christ. Our suffering can be redeemed and can help us and others identify with what Christ suffered for us.

Joy is so much more than a happy countenance. Happiness is temporary and based on circumstances. The presence of joy, on the other hand, indicates deep and mature character established by the Holy Spirit. Its presence is certainly visible in good times but even more so in challenging and difficult moments.[33] In the Hellenistic world, joy was a commonly used word that people tried to express through their actions. In the Greco-Roman empire, people sought to acquire joy through their circumstances and experiences, like postmodern, twenty-first century Western cultures. However, these sources of joy always fall short. For Christian leaders who are in Christ and walking in the Spirit, joy is a greater response—one not connected to the circumstances of life, but to "righteousness," "peace," and "hope" (Rom. 14:17; 15:13; 32–33).[34] When joy is not based on circumstances but on life in the Spirit, leaders can maintain a life of peace and hope no matter the situations in which they find themselves.

Character Development

The Holy Spirit is responsible for developing biblical joy in our character. There will be times where we suffer painful experiences (2 Cor. 1:8). We may experience many temptations (Heb. 2:18) or not understand our overwhelming circumstances (James 1:2–5). In these difficult times, we must not forget that we are called according to God's purpose (Rom. 8:28). As we faithfully pursue God's character, the Holy Spirit uses our circumstances to develop joy in us.[35]

In Luke 15:8–12, Jesus teaches about what brings true joy through the parable of the lost coin. A woman loses a precious coin, and she searches desperately to find it. After much searching, she finds the coin. In her joy, she invites her friends and neighbors to experience her joy with her. Jesus says that in the same way, the angels in heaven are full of joy when the lost are found.

This parable demonstrates how committed we can be to reaching our desired goals. In the woman's case, her goal was joy, and attaining that required effort and dedication on her part. At times, we may feel like we are lost causes, but we must commit to enduring through difficult situations to achieve our desired results. This parable has eternal significance, as it illustrates our souls being found and coming alive in Christ. As we look at every situation in life through this lens, we come to understand that biblical joy arises from godly character.

The Early Church

In the early church, believers expressed joy in many ways and through a variety of circumstances. Joy filled the city of Samaria while Philip preached, as evil spirits left people (Acts 8:8). Joy came to the Ethiopian eunuch when Philip explained to him what he was reading in the prophet Isaiah. Philip baptized the eunuch in water, and the man went away rejoicing (Acts 8:38). As John B. Polhill imagines, "The eunuch continued southward on his long journey home. Somehow it did not seem so arduous. He was filled with joy, a genuine manifestation of the Spirit's work in his life."[36] Joy came to the jailer and his entire household after being led to faith in Jesus by Paul and Silas (Acts 16:34). Ben Witherington III states:

> Out of gratitude the jailor immediately took the two evangelists and washed their wounds, and in turn was washed by them, the jailor and his whole family being baptized on the spot. V. 34 indicates that the jailor also brought the two into his own house and set food before them. It was a joyous feast, the whole household celebrating the jailor becoming a believer in the true God.[37]

In like manner, S. S. Smalley highlights the joy of the early church: "Joy marks the life of the early church, through which the rule of God is disclosed. The basis of the church's rejoicing is the death and resurrection of Jesus (Acts 2:26)."[38] Early Christians rejoiced when Gentiles became followers of Christ. In fact, there is more rejoicing in heaven when one sinner repents than over many righteous people who do not (Acts 15:3; Luke 15:7)[39]

Joy in Circumstances

People often hope that their situation in life will bring them joy. For most people, some circumstances in their lives are not joyful or joy-giving. Circumstances and situations change moment by moment and person to person. Christian leaders must find their joy beyond mere status, personality, possessions, or circumstances. Joy transcends these things and comes from real meaning and purpose. We can only find real joy when we belong to Christ and our relationships and circumstances are making an eternal difference.

CHAPTER 4

Peace

P EACE IS THE THIRD CHARACTERISTIC OF THE HOLY SPIRIT'S presence in the lives of believers. Peace is not the result a life without trials and trouble; rather, it is produced despite troubles and trials (Gal. 5:22). Paul contrasts the peace of life in the Spirit with the lack of peace in a life lived to gratify the flesh. Peace that gratifies the flesh is focused on the absence of conflict. Biblical peace is found when a person is in alignment with Christ through the Spirit.

The notion of peace is so prevalent in the New Testament that it is mentioned in every book, a total of eighty times.[40] The Greek word for peace (*eirene*) is more than a wish for goodwill and a life without conflict.[41] *Shalom,* the equivalent word in Hebrew, encompasses the notion that peace is more than the absence of war and trouble. A peaceful life is one of wholeness and prosperity.[42] It describes the condition of our inner spirit when conflict or trouble is present—our ability to respond with calm assurance in all circumstances.

Peace and Opposition

John 14:26–27 provides significant insight into peace. The Holy Spirit comes upon believers and teaches them all wisdom. He instructs believers in their hearts and minds, prompting them to obey His voice. John makes it clear that God's peace, which only comes from the Holy Spirit, is a peace the world cannot give. This peace does not exempt believers from difficulty. In fact, Jesus was troubled as He faced crucifixion, yet He spoke of peace that only comes from calm confidence in God. Jesus had this peace because He trusted and was confident in His Father's love and approval.[43] At the time of John's writings, the only peace that people understood was the peace that came from the protection of the Roman Empire. John was not writing about Roman peace, or any other government or system's peace but Holy Spirit peace that is constantly present in Holy Spirit–indwelt people despite oppression or opposition.[44]

I learned some of my earliest leadership lessons from watching my dad as he pastored our church growing up. One couple brought a great deal of opposition into his life, and he would speak about it at times. I could tell the couple was difficult for my dad to get along with, but after he would express his emotions for a moment, his face would light up with a grin and he would ask God for patience. This couple was very faithful. They sat three rows back on the right side of the auditorium on Sunday morning, Sunday evening, and Wednesday night. The wife was profoundly spiritual, expressing herself vocally during the service and uttering an occasional amen during the message. The husband was the exact opposite; he sat with a frown on his face, his arms crossed. When the congregation stood, he sat. Most challengingly, when my dad would open the Bible and start to preach, the man would open up the Sunday newspaper, pop it open with a loud snap, and hold it up to his face as he read the news. I remember many amusing stories about this couple, but mostly I remember my dad patiently loving them through some particularly challenging moments.

Despite persecution and imprisonment, Paul declared, "I have learned to be content whatever the circumstances" (Phil. 4:11). He fully embraced hardship, knowing that his external conditions could not affect the Spirit within him. As Christian leaders allow the Holy Spirit to develop internal peace within, their circumstances will no longer determine their attitude.

Paul fully understood the concept of possessing peace despite circumstances, and he encouraged his fellow believers to fully embrace the work of the Holy Spirit to experience this inner peace themselves. Paul urged his spiritual brothers and sisters in Philippi to "let the peace of God, which transcends all understanding, guard your hearts and minds in Christ Jesus" (Phil. 4:6, 7).[45] If we do not have God's Spirit at work in our lives, we cannot comprehend that it is possible to experience peace in the midst of turbulent times. This is what makes it a peace that surpasses understanding.

Change of Focus

Peace comes not through a change in circumstances, but through a shift in focus. Christian leaders who understand the power of the Holy Spirit's work will focus their attention upon that which provides real peace. Paul encouraged believers to let the peace of Christ rule in their hearts and to let the message of Christ dwell among them (Col. 3:12–17). Elaborating on this exhortation, Gordon Fee asserts that peace must be more relational than circumstantial:

> Peace is a community matter. That is, Paul's first concern with "peace" is not "the well-arranged heart"—although again, it is difficult to have "peace" in a community where God's people know little peace individually … God himself is often described as "the God of peace," the God who dwells in total *Shalom* (wholeness, well-being), and who gives such *Shalom* to his people in their life together.[46]

As he preached to the church in Galatia, Paul emphasized the inner work of Christ, encouraging the Jews and the Gentiles to understand God's message.[47] Leaders who put their energy into the work of Christ and their focus onto the Word of God will find true peace.

CHAPTER 5

Patience

THE GREEK WORD FOR PATIENCE, *MAKROTHYMIA*, IS DEFINED AS "long-suffering."[48] When we demonstrate patience, we keep our anger under control. A patient person does not get easily angered to begin with. Even when expressing righteous anger, it is to be done in a regulated way, addressing the reason for the anger without personal attacks. Paul referred to himself as the worst of sinners, recognizing that God, in His mercy, had been patient with Him (1 Tim. 1:16).[49] He saw himself as a recipient of Christ's "perfect patience," so that he could be an example that might bring others to eternal life.

The Human Response

Patience can also be called forbearance, which is patience specifically exercised toward other people. The definition of long-suffering is showing extended forbearance to those who cause you distress. As Fee notes:

One is "patient" about all kinds of very nonpersonal matters pertaining to life in general (computers that go haywire, for instance). But in Paul this noun and its corresponding verb are always used in contexts involving one's forbearance toward others. As such it often occurs, as it does here, as the passive side of love, of which its companion "kindness" is the active side.[50]

God exemplifies this attitude toward humanity as shown in Romans 2:4, showing forbearance and kindness in response to human arrogance. For us humans, developing that kind of patience is a result of the inner working of God's Spirit empowering us to put up with those who need love, kindness, and second, third, and fourth chances.[51] Here, it becomes apparent that Paul listed the character qualities of the fruit of the Spirit in an intentional order, because only a soul filled with love, joy, and peace is can be patient.

God Is Patient

God himself is our model of patience, as mentioned in 2 Peter 3:9. Peter seems to be referring to God's patience in Noah's time, since he referenced this account previously. God showed His patient nature by withholding judgment on people's wickedness (Gen. 3)[52]

Nehemiah 9 describes God's many demonstrations of patience toward Israel. He performed signs and wonders to free them from slavery in Egypt. At the Red Sea, He heard their cry and parted the waters. When they were hungry and thirsty, God provided food and water. Fulfilling His covenant promise to Abraham, He gave them a prosperous land and delivered kingdoms and nations into their hands (v. 22). Though God's mighty hand intervened for the Israelites time and time again, they responded with contempt and rebellion (v. 26). Yet God remained patient with them. Nehemiah says, "For many years You were patient with them. By Your Spirit You warned them ... but in Your great mercy, You did not put an end to them, for You are gracious and merciful" (Neh. 9:31).[53]

A Bigger Plan

To fully comprehend Spirit-given patience, we must understand that God intends for us to view life from a broad perspective. Often, we respond with impatience when things do not turn out as we hoped. However, if we learn to contextualize our life experiences within a wider view, our chances of overreacting to immediate circumstances are diminished, because we can recognize that God is working out a bigger plan. For a season of my life, I worked in a very unhealthy environment. At times, I begged God to give me a new assignment. The stress level was more than I thought I could stand. One night, as I lay awake in the early hours of the morning, not wanting to disturb anyone else in the house, I found my way to the bathroom and sat on the floor, crying out to God for an answer. The answer came, but I didn't know it at the time. God's response was, "Be patient; I have something for you to learn." Looking back, I see now that not only did I survive; more importantly, I grew. God saw things from a much more eternal perspective than I did, and I only needed to remain patient and trust that He had a bigger plan.

Proverbs observes that a "hot-tempered person stirs up conflict, but a patient one calms a quarrel" (Prov. 15:18). Likewise, Paul calls believers to "be patient with everyone" (1 Thess. 5:14). The biblical model for Holy Spirit–driven patience involves choosing grace and mercy over anger and resentment. Holy Spirit–driven character does not react in the moment but sees circumstances and people as long-term opportunities for God to work out His purpose and plan.

CHAPTER 6

Kindness

THE GREEK WORD FOR KINDNESS, *CHRESTOTES*, DESCRIBES God's gracious attitude and action toward sinners.[54] It can also reference the generosity of God. A Spirit-led person who exudes kindness displays gentleness, charm, peacefulness, and the ability to get along with all kinds of people. Kindness does not infer weakness but rather indicates a good heart that resembles the heart of God.[55] Jerry Bridges notes that goodness and kindness are closely connected, often interchangeable, character qualities:

> Kindness is a sincere desire for the happiness of others; goodness is the activity calculated to advance that happiness. Kindness is the inner disposition, created by the Holy Spirit, that causes us to be sensitive to the needs of others, whether physical, emotional, or spiritual. Goodness is kindness in action—words and deeds.[56]

When leaders demonstrate kindness, they exhibit a part of God's nature and show that the Spirit is active in their lives. The scriptures reinforce this aspect of God: "Taste and see that the Lord is good" (Ps. 34:8, 1 Pet. 2:3). Luke 6:36 declares: "Your reward will be great, and you will be children of the Most High, because He is kind to the ungrateful and wicked." Luke indicates that the character quality of kindness, which God demonstrates to humanity, should be shown to others. In so doing, believers demonstrate God's character.[57]

Christian Character

Believers reflect God's heart to humanity by embodying God's kindness. To fully understand kindness, we have only to look at the life of Jesus. When He encounters the woman with the issue of blood (Luke 8:42b-48), Jesus extends kindness. When she admitted that she touched Him, Jesus said, "Your faith has healed you" (v. 48). Jesus responded to her physical need but also addressed the bigger need—her soul. Biblical kindness involves improving physical circumstances for others and addressing the greater need for spiritual restoration.[58] Romans 4:2 declares: "God's kindness leads people to repentance."

When Jesus healed the woman, He did so with gentleness. Sometimes, we do physical acts of kindness with an attitude of frustration about the inconvenience a person is causing us. Grant Osborne states: "We must never look down upon or judge others when we ourselves are not right with God. We are all alike sinners before God, and in our condemnation of others we indict ourselves."[59] Jesus demonstrated a spirit of love in the way He spoke to the woman. He showed kindness by meeting both her spiritual and physical needs. In like manner, Christian leaders ought to express kindness with a caring attitude.[60]

When my son Kramer was six years old, our family traveled to Fairbanks, Alaska, with a college ministry team. We had limited space in our suitcases, so my wife and I asked Kramer to choose just a few of his favorite toys to take. These included a Star Wars X Wing Fighter, a Millennium Falcon, and several of his favorite action figures. It was early March, and the average temperature in Fairbanks was minus thirty degrees Fahrenheit. We purchased a new winter coat for Kramer to make sure he would be warm. In Alaska, we had the opportunity to minister to many people. One afternoon, we arranged to do an outreach at the Fairbanks Rescue Mission. As the team started setting up equipment, my wife and I noticed Kramer playing in the corner with a new friend. Within minutes, Kramer brought him over to meet us. His name was Tyler. Kramer said, "Mom and Dad, this is my new friend Tyler; he moved here from Florida and hasn't been outside for more than three months. He doesn't have a coat or toys. Would it be ok if I gave him my coat and a few of my Star Wars toys?"

What I had assumed would be a brief interaction was not what was in the heart of my young son. My wife agreed to Kramer's request, and we watched him hand over his brand-new coat and two of his most prized possessions to his new friend. We found a few sweatshirts in our luggage to wrap around Kramer and watched him and his new friend go out into the cold to play in the snow.

Tyler's parents came over and introduced themselves to us as the boys played. We found out that they had driven from Florida to Fairbanks for a promised job. By the time they arrived in Fairbanks, the job had been given to someone else. The family had spent everything they had to make the journey. It was winter, and very few jobs or housing were available, which is why they were living at the mission. We had a wonderful time getting to know the family, and before we left, we invited them to our next service.

Two days later, we were preparing for an evening service at True North Church and wondering if Tyler's family would come to the service. The service was getting ready to start, and Kramer, sitting on the front row with Brenda and me, leaned over and asked, "Dad, do you think Tyler will be here?" As the words came out of his mouth, I heard the back door of the church open, and in walked a young boy with Kramer's coat on, holding two Star Wars toys in his hands. Behind him were both his parents and more than a dozen people from the mission.

At the end of the service, the entire family stood and committed themselves to Christ, along with several others from the mission. Kramer's kindness met the physical needs of a young boy that day, but more importantly, it met the spiritual needs of a family and several of their friends. Kindness does, indeed, lead to repentance (Rom. 2:4).

Kindness with Purpose

The prophet Isaiah poignantly illustrates Jesus's kind nature: "Here is my servant … I will put my Spirit on him … He will not shout or cry out, or raise His voice in the streets. A bruised reed He will not break, and a smoldering wick He will not snuff out" (Isa. 42:1–3). Early Akkadian manuscripts shed light on the metaphor in this passage. The Assyrians had a practice of crushing any weak or disloyal people under their feet. Such people would be snapped "like a reed." In contrast, servants of Yahweh were not called to defeat or humiliate their opponents. Continuing the metaphor, the wick of an oil lamp is an essential element for light, but if it is only smoldering, it is tossed away as useless. In contrast, we believers serve a God whose character is kind. He never tosses us to the side but continually gives us value, purpose, and usefulness.[61]

Modern American culture needs the message of this passage. In our culture, if an individual expresses weakness, his or her opponents will expose it and use it for their own personal advantage. Taking advantage of the weak is not the way of the Spirit-led life. Leaders guided by the Spirit see potential in people, especially those whom they might have the opportunity to influence toward a relationship with God. Even when other people do not act with kindness toward us, we have a responsibility to respond with kindness toward them. Jesus models an attitude of grace and second chances.

CHAPTER 7

Goodness

THE GREEK WORD FOR GOODNESS IS *AGATHOSYNE*. THIS RARE word combines both the doing and the being aspects of goodness. Leaders who possesses this quality are good in that they possess moral excellence.[62] In scripture, goodness sometimes appears as a synonym for the word *kindness*.[63] Because it is closely associated with kindness, it carries a similar meaning. The most common expression of goodness is generosity.[64] Throughout Galatians, Paul uses the word *goodness* to refer to God's generosity toward those found in Christ.

Developing Goodness

We often find ourselves fighting an internal battle against selfishness and sin. Although we may not welcome the idea of this fight, it is good to become aware of it. Recognizing this internal battle indicates that goodness is already at work in our lives. The Bible explains that "the mind governed by the flesh is hostile toward God" (Rom. 8:7). As Christian leaders focus their minds upon the good and generous qualities of God, they develop godly character that enables them to resist the natural tendency to defy God and entertain sin. God desires to help us overcome this tendency and to empower us to live a life of righteousness and goodness. Paul includes goodness among the fruit of the Spirit in contrast to his preceding list of acts of the flesh (Gal. 5:19–21). He emphasizes that those who sow to the Spirit do good for others from a heart of generosity, rather than for selfish personal gain.[65]

The entirety of scripture reveals the generosity of God. The psalmist expresses the beautiful reality that God's goodness and love follow His children all the days of their lives (Ps. 23:6). Every day and in every situation, God's Spirit is eager to pour goodness and abundance into the lives of those who seek Him (Ps. 65:11). God wants to demonstrate His goodness toward those who focus their minds on righteousness, but His goodness does not stop there. God's goodness also refers to His mercy and patience, which He gives in generous measure to bring people to repentance (Rom. 2:4).[66]

Doing Good Works Does Not Mean Being Saved

God intends for His followers to be "fruit bearers" (John 15:8). God desires His children to actively do good things, just as Jesus did. Acts 10:38 indicates that Jesus was filled with the Holy Spirit and did good things such as healing people (Acts 10:38). He embodied the Spirit and gave that same Spirit to us, empowering us to walk in obedience (Acts 5:32). However, doing good works does not mean we are saved by them. God reconciles us solely by His grace—the generous "gift of God" (Eph. 2:8). Christian leaders who fully understand the grace given to them by God will gladly fulfill

God's command to do good works for others (2 John 1:6). The greatest part of leadership is serving people, not for the attainment of salvation, but rather as evidence of salvation. Leaders should extend the grace they have received from God to other people.

While pastoring in Seattle, my wife and I lived next door to two women who were in a committed relationship with one another. They assumed that since I was a pastor, I would judge them for their lifestyle. To be clear, I do believe there is a biblical standard for marriage, but it is difficult to hold others to that standard if they do not believe in the authority of scripture. One day I was outside mowing my lawn and one of the women jokingly shouted to me, "When you're done with your lawn, go ahead and mow ours!" Her tone was cynical, and I knew she thought I would never do that for such a person as her. Then I saw the women get into their car and head out for the afternoon. I felt the Lord drop a thought in my heart: "You are called to serve people as evidence of your salvation, not for the attainment of salvation." For the next two hours, I mowed their lawn, edged their driveway, and swept their walkways. When they returned home, they came and knocked on my door to thank me. They told me directly that they never thought someone like me would ever do something for people like them. The next time they left for vacation, they gave me a key to their house and asked if I would feed their cats. Of course, I said yes, and I mowed their lawn again. Many conversations emerged from that experience as the Holy Spirit built a beautiful bridge in our friendship.

Doing Good to the Hateful

One of the most difficult commands of God is to "do good to those who hate you" (Luke 6:27). Responding to hatred with goodness is also one of the most challenging aspects of leadership. Pouring out goodness and blessings on offensive, mean-spirited, and spiteful people is not easy, yet Jesus expands this commandment even more, teaching that "it is no credit to you if you only do good to those who are good to you, even sinners love those who love them back" (Luke 6:32). Paul told the Galatians that they should do good to everyone, especially those who are believers (Gal. 6:10). The emphasis is on the word *everyone*. The fruit of goodness should be lavished on all people, regardless of whether they return the favor. As Udo Schnelle says:

> Christians should attempt to do good always and for everyone but especially for their brothers and sisters of the Christian community. The love of brothers and sisters within the family of God is the mark of Christian existence. The Christian brother or sister imposes a limit on one's own actions, for where their freedom begins, there one's own freedom ends.[67]

As we Christian leaders show goodness to other people, it is crucial that we examine the motives of our hearts. If our motivation is to be seen as highly spiritual, our reward from God will be nullified (Matt. 6:1–4). However, if our good deeds are done to bring glory to God, we are truly being a light to the world (Matt. 5:16).

Paul's closing statement in Romans 15 contains a powerful message about goodness. He encourages the church in Antioch to be ministers to the Gentiles (everyone) as an example of the generous grace God has already given to them. He reminds them of their priestly duty to "proclaim the gospel" (goodness builds God's kingdom) so that the Gentiles (everyone) might be sanctified (saved) by the Holy Spirit. Donald Gee writes about the importance and impact of goodness:

Goodness can be the consolation and reward of those who may never be conspicuous for brilliant gifts. Dorcas was no prophetess like Deborah, or even the daughters of Philip, but the fact she "was always doing good and helping the poor" has been recorded for the inspiration of Christian womanhood all down the ages (Acts 9: 36). In Barnabas, this particular fruit of the Spirit appeared in such prominence and richness that it is recorded of him: "He was a good man, full of the Holy Spirit and faith, and a great number of people were brought to the Lord" (Acts 11: 24). May God give His Church many more such pastors as the first one with whom the privileged assembly at Antioch was blessed.[68]

It is out of the good that is done for another that the love of Christ is revealed. People are drawn to Christ through acts of kindness that are performed without expected reciprocation.

CHAPTER 8

Faithfulness

FAITHFULNESS IS THE QUALITY OF BEING TRUSTWORTHY AND reliable. The Greek word *pistis*, translated as faithfulness, is the state of being one in whom others can have complete confidence. Leaders can put their faith in a person who is trustworthy and reliable.[69] Likewise, believers can put their faith and confidence in leaders who are proven faithful.

God is the best example of faithfulness. "If we are faithless, He remains faithful, for He cannot disown Himself" (2 Tim. 2:13). God's very nature embodies the character quality of faithfulness. Additionally, God's Word is right and true, and He is faithful in all that He does (Ps. 33:4). Therefore, believers can hold onto the promised hope found in God because He does what He says He will do (Heb. 10:23). Paul writes, "Can the 'unfaithfulness' of God's people nullify the 'faithfulness' of God?" (Rom. 3:3). The answer is no. God is still faithful (pistis) even when people are not faithful.

Romans 3:3 can be interpreted as a reference to God's

faithfulness to believers, but most likely, it was intended to be a personal exhortation to believers to remain faithful to God. The fruit of faithfulness is born from trusting God in all circumstances. Leaders often go through hard times, endure seasons of doubt, and face persecution. Paul suggests that with the Spirit present in our lives, we will be empowered to remain faithful and trust God unwaveringly.[70]

Faithfulness of Abraham

Abraham was called God's friend because God could count on him to be faithful in all He asked him to do. Abraham was zealous about carrying out God's instructions even when he did not understand them (James 2:23). Genesis indicates that Abraham believed (*pisteuo*) the Lord, and the Lord saw him as righteous. Abraham took the Lord at His word and responded faithfully, without questioning. In response, God saw him as righteous, not because of what Abraham did, but because of his trust in God's promises. Paul used the story of Abraham to demonstrate his message to the Galatians: "Abraham believed God, and God saw him as righteous" (Gal. 3:6). Even after Abraham's death, God's referred to him as one who obeyed His voice and kept His commandments (Gen. 26:3–5). Because of these acts of obedience, God committed His promises to Abraham and his son Isaac (22:16). God said, "Because you have acted faithfully in the giving of your son and you have obeyed My voice, I will make your descendants as numerous as the stars and bless them."[71]

The significance of Abraham's faithfulness and its connection to the promises of the Abrahamic covenant are still valid today under the new covenant. George P. Kimber comments on the continuity of God's Word through all generations:

It is unfortunate that in some circles of Christianity, there is a tendency to relegate some of the promises of the Scriptures only relevant to past generations and not applicable to the present. God's covenant with Abraham and his descendants was not just for the rest of the Old Testament, but the whole New Testament. The covenant included a reference to "all the families of the earth" (Gen. 12:1–3; 17:7). Only now in Christ have these promises begun to be fulfilled, for Jesus Christ and His people are the true seed of Abraham (Gal. 3:29). The final fulfillment lies beyond history. Then Abraham's seed will be a great multitude that no one can count, and their inheritance will be the New Jerusalem (Gen. 22:17; Heb. 11:8–12, 16, 39, 40; Rev. 7:9).[72]

Even now, God is faithfully fulfilling His promise to Abraham in the lives of believer's today. God's Spirit worked in Abraham's life in the same way that He works in the lives of Christian leaders today, molding and shaping their character and enabling them to be faithful followers of Jesus and effective leaders of His church.

The Disciples

The Jewish philosopher Philo (c. 20 BCE–AD 40) based his entire philosophical worldview on his perception of Jesus. Philo combined Greek philosophical concepts with Hebrew religious thought to develop a platform for the conception of Christian ideals. Philo concluded that when Jesus called His disciples "friends," He was not just referring to a transactional association between master and servant, but rather to a relationship of deep faithfulness, built upon trust, respect, and intimacy (John 15:15).[73]

Peter and John had this kind of relationship with Jesus, which produced a great amount of faith. They put their faith into action when they met the lame beggar at the temple gate (Acts 3:1–10). When Peter saw the man, he reached out and took his hand with unwavering confidence. By faith, Peter and John believed the man would be healed and thus faithfully pronounced his healing. The man's life was changed that day, but the story's focus is more on the faithful action of the disciples.[74] The commitment that they made to follow Jesus that day indicates that their actions were led by the Spirit.

Sometimes, ministry leaders feel that they are called to serve a particular person or a particular pastor, but they are called to serve God. Whether the context of our leadership is a school, a church, a business, or another specific vocation, the true calling of disciples is faithfulness. There are seasons of our lives where faithfulness looks like being a student, a spouse, a parent, a teacher, a pastor, or a businessperson. God's call is to respond faithfully when our assignment arrives, the same way that Peter and John responded to the man at the temple.

My son-in-law taught me an amazing lesson in faithfulness. Jared is a fabulous leader and communicator. In May 2019, Jared was twenty-eight years old, and he and my daughter, Kaitlyn, had been married for nearly six years. He was serving as the executive teaching pastor at Canvas Church in Montana. Together, he and Kaitlyn had big dreams of planting a church in Billings, Montana, starting a family, and making an impact together.

One day, my wife Brenda and I were on the road, beginning a weekend away to celebrate the completion of a great and successful year at Northwest University. As we drove, Brenda received a phone call from Kaitlyn. I could hear my daughter's voice coming through the phone. She was in a state of hysteria and shock as she screamed, "They just diagnosed Jared with cancer!" We immediately changed our plans and drove nine hours to the hospital in Montana.

The next few days were filled with uncertainty as doctors discovered a rapidly growing eight-inch mass in Jared's chest and made plans for him to move to Seattle for advanced treatment. The ultimate diagnosis came back as acute lymphoblastic leukemia, which is most often found in young children. After reorganizing what "normal" looked like for our family and getting the treatment process started, Jared spoke to our students at Northwest University the following fall semester about his journey.

His life story and the testimony he gave has changed my understanding of what it means to be a disciple called to kingdom work. He said, "God called me to give Him my life, and I will be as faithful to that calling in life as I am in death. A medical diagnosis will not change the plan and purpose God has for me." Today, Jared's prognosis is favorable, and he and Kaitlyn are on their way to planting that church in Billings. I am so thankful that his story has already made an impact on so many, including me. God calls His disciples to faithfulness in every season of their lives.

Stewardship

In the parable of the talents (Matt. 25:14–30), Jesus shows two examples of people who were faithful with their talents and one who was not. The person who was not faithful lost the talent with which he had been entrusted. The individuals who were faithful performed their duties based on the trust and respect they had for the owner. They knew the owner well enough to know his intentions and chose to not only protect his investment but to make it grow.[75] In the same way, the owner knew his servants well enough to entrust them with his investment. The trust was reciprocal. Those who knew the owner best performed their duties well and built their credibility. Because of their faithfulness, these individuals were blessed further and entrusted with future opportunities (v. 20).

Christian leaders who invest in a committed relationship with God will grow in faithfulness. When we experience the faithfulness of God in our life circumstances, our faith grows. In response, our faithfulness toward God also grows. Both Abraham and Jesus's disciples became more faithful, developed intimacy with God, and believed in His faithfulness.

CHAPTER 9

Gentleness

ENTLENESS IS A FRUIT OF THE SPIRIT THAT IS ESSENTIAL FOR building and maintaining relationships. Leaders who display the character quality of gentleness demonstrate an even temper, an unpretentious attitude, and controlled passion. Gentleness comes from the Greek word *praos* and typically describes a person who possesses both strength and calmness.[76] R. E. Ciampa reflects upon the significant role of gentleness in leaders today:

> Jesus taught that leadership among his disciples was to be quite different from that in the world (Mark 10:42–45), more a matter of suffering and service than of power and authority. Timothy is exhorted to strive for gentleness (1 Tim. 6:11), and it is an essential qualification for the office of bishop or overseer (1 Tim. 3:3). Leaders have to communicate, and gentleness makes communication more effective.[77]

We should not mistake the spirit of gentleness for weakness; it takes real strength to be a gentle leader. People tend to hold in high esteem leaders who display this characteristic. It takes God's power at work in us to produce the character quality of gentleness.

For a season, I had the distinct privilege of working with one of my greatest mentors, Dr. Warren Bullock, who served as the superintendent of the Assemblies of God Northwest Ministry. Dr. Bullock is a gifted leader who embodies both strength and gentleness. During the time I worked with him, the Ministry Network underwent a significant financial crisis, and he was the leader chosen to guide more than thirteen hundred ministers through this difficult season. The situation was challenging for everyone to navigate, and we tried to build morale among leaders while digging the network out of severe economic circumstances. One afternoon, we were strategizing about how to host a ministers' lunch. We wanted to give a small gift to the ministers as a token of appreciation for their support in a tough time. Of course, the budget was already tight, and we were calling in every favor we could think of to make the event successful. During our planning, I offered a suggestion. Having lived in Seattle for many years, I had established a relationship with a developing coffee company, and I hoped they might help our cause. I suggested to Dr. Bullock that I give my friends a call and see if the company would make a deal. After all, every pastor would love a pound of coffee, and it would be great publicity for this new business. I called my friends, and the response over the phone was better than I could have hoped for. I ordered enough coffee for all the attendees, and we were excited about our gift.

The event went well, and as I had anticipated, the coffee was a huge success. A few days later, I received an invoice from the coffee company. When I opened the envelope, my heart sank. The bill was five times the amount I had heard my friend quote over the phone. I broke out into a sweat, and my hands began to shake. I called my friend at the company, and when I asked her about the amount, she laughed and said, "There is no way we could have quoted you what you thought you heard. It is impossible to sell our coffee to you for that amount. The invoice is the amount we quoted you, and we need you to pay it." My mistake, of course, was trusting a verbal quote without getting it in writing. The walk down the hall that day to Dr. Bullock's office felt like an eternity. I knew and respected how hard he had worked to fix the network's financial crisis, and I did not want to disappoint him. I showed him the invoice. After apologizing and explaining what I did wrong, he said, "Well, this will likely be one of the most expensive lessons you will ever learn, and I'll bet you won't do this again." He got up from his desk, gave me a pat on the back, and assured me that we would figure this out together. While other leaders might have yelled, spoken shaming words, or, worse, fired me, Dr. Bullock taught me what the fruit of the Spirit of gentle strength looks like in a leader.

Zechariah 9:9 depicts God as gentle. In this passage, the prophet is announcing the coming of Zion's King. In ancient days, kings would ride into a city on a horse or in a chariot, displaying their military power and royal majesty. On the contrary, Zechariah says that Zion's King would come on a donkey, demonstrating humility and peace. Even a mule would have been more regal, but this King chose to arrive on the lowest animal. The King of Zion is coming without any pomp and circumstances but rather with meekness and humility.[78]

Matthew 11:29 continues this theme of meekness and humility. Jesus calls His followers to "take my yoke upon you." This image of putting on a tool worn by a beast of labor implies that the disciples' lives would require humility. At that time, people of low status used a yoke to pull heavy loads. In this passage, the yoke refers to slavery or total submission to the master. God does not force His yoke upon us as slaves but rather invites us to take it up voluntarily. Jesus requests for His disciples to submit to the lowly posture that is inherent in God's law so that we can find rest for our souls.[79]

Paul made a statement about the gentle character of Christ when he appealed to the church in Corinth: "By the humility and gentleness of Christ, I appeal to you" (2 Cor. 10:1). Paul had a reputation for writing and teaching with boldness and confidence, but when he was physically present with fellow Christians, he had a more restrained demeanor. Paul was not afraid to strongly correct believers, but he preferred to take the more gentle approach that resembled Christ.[80]

The word *gentle* in Matthew 11:29 more accurately means "restful": "Come to me ... and I will rest you ... for I am restful ... and you will find rest for your soul." D. A. Carson expounds on this idea:

> On "rest" (*anapausis*, GK 398), see v. 28. Here the words "and you will find rest for your souls" are directly quoted from Jeremiah 6:16. The entire verse is steeped in OT language; but if this is intended to be not just an allusion but a fulfillment passage, then Jesus is saying that "the ancient paths" and "the good way" (Jer. 6:16) lie in taking on his yoke because he is the one to whom the OT Scriptures point. That yoke is "easy" ("good," "comfortable," GK 5982), and his burden is light (v. 30). The "rest" he promises is not only for the world to come but also for this one as well.[81]

A person who is gentle in spirit is one who has found rest in Christ—not only rest to come in eternity but also the rest available to him or her now through a deepening relationship with Christ.

In keeping with Christ's character and example, we can easily reimagine Paul's remarks in 2 Corinthians 10:1 as saying: "Acting as Christ would act, I appeal to you." Paul was not demanding or insisting. He presented his request with a sense of urgency while aligning himself with the known character of Christ. He wanted the Corinthians to know his sincere and caring heart for them.

Paul references Christ's character of gentleness in Philippians 2:5: "In your relationships with one another, have the same mindset as Christ." Jesus's humility is an encouragement to believers to follow His example. Christian leaders must aim to possess the same gentle spirit as Jesus to establish receptive relationships with those they hope to influence.

CHAPTER 10

Self-Control

I N THE GREEK, "SELF-CONTROL" COMES FROM THE WORD *enkrateia*. This is a two-part word: *en* means "in" and *krateia* means "power" (in-power).[82] Dunn reflects further on this idea:

> The concept is almost wholly absent from the Hebrew Bible, though it appears (chiefly) in the Wisdom literature of Hellenistic Judaism, and Josephus claims that it was held in high regard by the Essenes (*War ii.120*). NT usage reflects the same feature; the word appears nowhere in the Gospels, and the noun elsewhere only in Acts 24:25 and 2 Peter 1:6, though it appears more regularly in second-century's Christian writings.[83]

In Acts 24:25, Paul was on trial for preaching about the resurrection of the dead. When Felix visited Paul in prison a few days later, Paul talked to him about righteousness (right-living) and self-control (en krateia). As a result of this conversation, Felix became afraid and left Paul in jail for two more years.

In 2 Peter 1:6, Peter lists several character qualities that resemble the Galatians 5 fruit of the Spirit. He says that to live a godly life, believers must rely on "divine power," which they acquire through the Holy Spirit. Peter catalogues eight character qualities: faith, goodness, knowledge, self-control, perseverance, godliness, mutual affection, and love. Interestingly, the eight qualities build upon one another, demonstrating that growing in godly knowledge and behavior is a process.

Another key verse that fleshes out the meaning of self-control is Titus 1:8, which outlines the required character qualities of elders or overseers of the church. In these highly visible leadership roles, people must demonstrate advanced character development. In this passage, Paul states that such people should be self-controlled, upright, holy, and disciplined.[84]

The Opposite of Self-Control

To understand the meaning of self-control, we must identify who is in power. Paul's message is clear: God must be the one in control for leaders to have character qualities that show real Christian living and leadership. Leaders must develop the ability to abstain from the ungodly pleasures of this world. This commitment enables them to experience and understand the strength that God's Spirit provides to overcome temptation.

The opposite of self-control is self-indulgence. Matthew uses adamant language to address hypocritical leaders who project a persona of cleanliness but in reality are full of greed and self-indulgence (akrasi) (Matt. 23:25). The word akrasi refers to the quality of lacking self-control.[85] Timothy also spoke of this character trait, using a similar word (akrates). This word describes the inability to keep passions under control (2 Tim. 3:3).[86] For example, Paul encourages unmarried people who lack the ability to control their passions to get married (1 Cor. 7:9).[87]

Self-Control and the Mind

Getting married as a means of dealing with a lack of self-control can be the answer for some people, but it has also proven to be disastrous for others. Creating the opportunity for sexual passion does not necessarily rid a person of immoderate sexual desire. The wisdom of Proverbs offers good advice: godly people are encouraged to guard their hearts, for the heart is the wellspring of life (Prov. 4:23). The heart includes the mind and all that comes from within. When sin occurs, it happens twice: once in the mind and once again in action. Thus, the development of self-control starts with a mind centered on God. As R. Scott Sullender says, "Understanding sin as addiction helps us see, as Jesus suggested in the Sermon on the Mount, that sin begins in the mind. There is a continuing between thought and deed."[88] As a person feeds unhealthy thoughts, the thought will become active. Thoughts and actions are connected, and one will certainly lead to the next unless the obsession is controlled and stopped.

Ministry leaders must develop self-control in the area of sexuality. We live in a world where addiction has become normative. The lure of sexual addiction is consuming. The pornography industry is taking advantage of people and feeding other sectors, including human trafficking. What makes this addiction especially difficult is how easily accessible pornography has become. All one needs is a smartphone and a photo to give the brain a dopamine dump from the limbic system. A pornography addict might get rid of his or her smartphone, but the images from that time of addiction will be filed in the memory for years to come, ready to be accessed at any moment by a trigger.

Over the years, my wife and I have counseled many young people who struggle with sexual addictions. If we had to choose only one major area that we have prayed about the most with young people, this would be it. Christian students easily get swept up in this addiction, and it can usually be effectively hidden, as opposed to other addictive substances like alcohol or drugs.

One day a young man asked to meet with me. We set an appointment, and he came to my office. This young person came from a decent home and had just become a believer. He opened our meeting with a shocking statement: "I did not realize pornography was bad, or even a sin." I asked him to explain. He went on to tell me that from the time he was five years old, his dad would share a daily pornographic picture with him. They would generally laugh and talk about the photo, generating some sort of "male bonding" experience. He said, "Even this morning, before meeting with you, I received an image from him." We talked about many things, including his distorted image of women and what it means to be a man. We talked about his future and what God was calling him to, and how he had this addiction that would not let him go. The young man tried everything. He had friends come around him, but they only served as people to whom he confessed, rather than providing real accountability.

Finally, out of desperation, he said he would be willing to do anything to get rid of this addiction. After praying for clarity about his next steps, I asked him where he viewed the images. He told me the viewing always occurred when he was by himself on his digital devices. I asked him if he would be willing to get rid of them. Within thirty minutes, he was standing at my door holding his computer and electronic devices. For the next few years, they sat on my office floor. He completed every one of his assignments in the open on public computers in the campus library. My friend graduated with a degree, but more than that, he graduated from his addiction to pornography. For the next ten years, he served faithfully as a staff pastor without returning to his previous addiction. He recently graduated with a master's degree and continues to fulfill God's call on his life.

The mind plays terrible tricks on us, and too often, it will lead us into areas we never intended to go if it is not intentionally controlled. Leaders can overcome temptation and develop self-control by implementing the following suggestions. First, read God's Word. This enables you to recognize temptations that oppose scripture. Jesus himself overcame temptation with scripture, and in so doing, He remained faithful to godly principles (Matt. 4). Russell Moore agrees with employing scripture to overcome temptation: "We resist temptation the way Jesus did, through the word of the kingdom. As we follow Jesus, we see the gospel reclaim our identity, reorder our desires and reframe our future."[89]

Second, feed your soul through prayer and fellowship with the Holy Spirit. In His moment of greatest difficulty, Jesus went off to a quiet place to pray so that He would not fall into temptation (Matt. 26:41). Prayer involves both speaking to and listening to the Spirit of God.

Third, keep your mind free from sinful input. Current culture is saturated with opportunities for temptation. Moore states: "The 'mind' in scripture is not chiefly your cognitive capacity, as though storing up memorized Bible verses for the purpose of information could stave off temptation. It is instead the core of your ability to perceive. That is intellectual, yes, to some degree, but also intuitive, personal, emotional, and imaginative."[90] Job made a commitment to purity and self-control when he declared, "I have made a covenant with my eyes not to look lustfully at a woman" (Job 31:1). Believers of both genders must make a commitment like this.

Fourth, find a person who will provide godly counsel and accountability. Hebrews 10:25 encourages believers to consider how to spur one another on to love and good deeds (Heb. 10:24–25). The inference in this passage is that believers should have a godly jealousy for righteousness, both in themselves and in other believers. A friend who will provide accountability and give honest and forthright feedback is crucial for developing self-control.[91]

Conclusion

As Paul concludes the list of essential character qualities, or fruit of the Spirit, that grow in Spirit-led believers, he intentionally ends with a character quality that refers to an earlier list in Galatians. In Galatians 5:19, Paul records fifteen areas of sin from which believers should abstain. To do so, they must draw from God's power. The fruit of the Spirit begins with love and ends with self-control, suggesting that love is the fundamental building block of character, while self-control is the mortar that joins all the other qualities together upon this foundation.

When we love people the way God does, the outcome is joy. When joy is present, peace begins to fill our lives. When love, joy, and peace are present, we more naturally express patience toward other people. When we exude the characteristics of love, joy, peace, and patience, it is to be expected that we would emanate kindness. As we build this life of character, self-control holds all the fruit in perfect balance, along with God's generous help.

Spirit-Led Character Development

CHARACTER DEVELOPMENT IS A LIFELONG PURSUIT. AS WE embrace the Holy Spirit's inner work, our character begins to bear the Spirit's fruit. Believers produce fruit by remaining connected to the vine, which is Jesus, and submitting to the pruning process of the gardener, who is God (John 15:5). In gardening, the growth process begins with cultivating good soil, creating the optimal conditions for healthy growth. A similar process occurs in human character development. The cultivation of the soil of character starts in the formative years of life, from toddler to around thirteen years old.[92] The foundation for a lifetime of character growth is laid during these formative years.

One of the greatest responsibilities parents and community members have is ensuring that children are exposed to biblical principles and that they witness models of godly living at an early age. This exposure helps children establish a healthy life, teaches them the practice of soul care, and prepares them for eternity. Christ followers must embrace their responsibility to raise godly children (Prov. 22:6). God's intention is for parents, family members, and community leaders to all be involved in laying a healthy foundation that prepares children to grow into healthy, productive, life-giving members of their communities.[93]

The next few chapters will introduce a spiritual formation process intended to lay the necessary groundwork for character development. Furthermore, they present specific character qualities that are outcomes of this formation process, connecting these characteristics to the fruit of the Spirit found in Galatians 5:22–23.

CHAPTER 11

Foundational Formation Process

DEVELOPMENT FOR ANY INDIVIDUAL—WHETHER PHYSICAL, mental, emotional, or spiritual—must be an intentional process. As living, organic beings, God created people to think, grow, and develop. If we do not approach our development intentionally, we will still grow unintentionally, perhaps resulting in unhealthy formation and dysfunction.[94]

Just as a child grows developmentally, so people grow spiritually. The initial steps occur as the Holy Spirit and influential people work in tandem to draw us toward a relationship with Christ. As the process continues, we choose to follow Christ and begin the process of personal growth in Him. During the personal growth step, we develop daily habits of Bible reading and prayer. Next, the relational growth step reintroduces the need for wise spiritual mentoring. The congregational step emphasizes the need for church involvement, and finally, the missional step fosters a mindset wherein we desire for other people to come to Christ, and we want to be involved in discipling these people, replicating the spiritual formation process in the lives of others.

The chart below depicts this spiritual formation process:

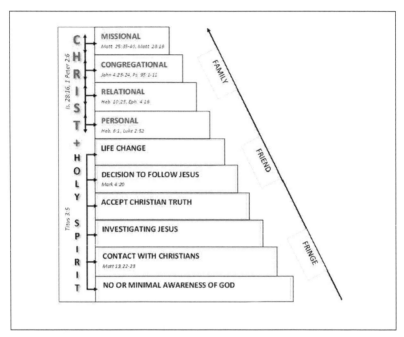

The process of spiritual formation is connected to believers' character development. When we commit to this process, the Holy Spirit's work in us bears spiritual fruit. I have developed a list of twenty-six character outcomes ideally seen in the life of a Christian leader and paired them with nine different leadership qualities that are connected to the fruit of the Spirit, as depicted in the following table:

Fruit of the Spirit	Leadership Quality	Character Outcomes
Love	Emotionally stable	Forgiving Courageous Possessing strong friendships Reverent
Joy	Positive in attitude	Grateful Enthusiastic
Peace	Self-assured	Content Confident Wise
Patience	Tough-minded	Humble Available Attentive
Kindness	Empathetic	Fair Generous Encouraging
Goodness	Mature	Honest Pure
Faithfulness	Team-oriented	Dependable Taking initiative Diligent
Gentleness	Conscientious	Compassionate Thoughtful Discrete
Self-control	Disciplined	Responsible Efficient Obedient

We must keep the character development process at the forefront of our vision as we learn to allow the Holy Spirit to grow fruit in us. Developing the leadership outcomes listed above might happen quickly for some of us. For others, they might take a lifetime to develop. What is important is our commitment to the process.

CHAPTER 12

Love and Emotional Stability

LOVE IS THE FOUNDATION OF ALL TWENTY-SIX CHARACTER outcomes. Paul says that love should be put on over all the virtues, as it is the fruit that binds all the others together in perfect unity (Col. 3:14). The character quality of emotional stability is connected to the fruit of love in a Spirit-guided leader.

Love can be defined as building up and meeting the needs of another person without expecting anything in return. Judith K. Balswick and Jack O. Balswick highlight the active nature of love: "Love is an art to be practiced, and it requires discipline, concentration, patience and supreme concern. When people start 'working at love,' the noticeable active elements will include behaviors like giving, caring, responsibility, respect and knowledge."[95] When Jesus washed His disciples' feet, He modeled what it means to love (John 13:1–17). Judas had already betrayed Him, but instead of showing anger, Jesus expressed love. He demonstrated real love, even though He was about to be betrayed, denied, and crucified. Scripture says it this way: "Jesus knew the hour had come for Him to leave this world and go to the Father. Having loved His own who were in the world, He loved them to the end" (v. 1).

To express love even when it is countercultural, we must be fully aware of and in control of our emotions. This requires emotional stability. An emotionally stable leader can determine the best response to a situation, even when that response contradicts his or her initial emotional reaction. A loving response does not necessarily mean no response; instead, it is a response that turns the circumstances into something better than they were originally.[96] Solomon wisely said, "Fools give full vent to their rage, but the wise bring calm in the end" (Prov. 29:11).

Leadership Quality: Emotional Stability

The topic of emotional stability has been extensively studied. Research indicates that understanding our emotional responses is more important than knowing our IQ.[97] Emotional stability and the ability to handle our feelings determine our success and happiness in all walks of life. Emotional stability includes the ability to control impulses, delay gratification, and self-motivate, as well as read people's social cues and handle the ups and downs of life.

William M. Struther's research indicates that the neurological circuitry responsible for intellect and the system responsible for emotion are interwoven.[98] For example, when an emergency occurs, the emotional center, or the limbic system, takes over the rest of the brain. This physiological takeover prompts us to fight, flee, or freeze. The amygdala, the portion of the brain that triggers emotion, is a limbic brain structure. It remains constantly alert to emergency situations and has the capacity to take over the rational center of the neocortex when action is needed. Emotions such as jealousy, pride, contempt, and fear, as well as other disorders such as hypersexuality from viewing pornography, posttraumatic stress, and anxiety disorders, affect rational processing because the active amygdala is doing its job to navigate perceived emotional threats.[99] When we are, for example, facing political dynamics in the workplace or navigating a domestic dispute, the amygdala begins to take over the prefrontal area of the brain, which is the executive processing center. The prefrontal cortex analyzes the information from all parts of the brain and makes decisions regarding responses. Without a prefrontal filter, emotional hijacking can result, wherein the amygdala reacts excessively and inappropriately to the circumstances. The prefrontal zone circuitry has failed to keep emotional impulses in check.[100]

Emotional stability and emotional competency are increasingly important for today's leadership.[101] Understanding the function of the brain is key to controlling our emotional responses to circumstances. As leaders react to daily operations, it is imperative to organizational and relational health that they can maintain healthy emotional responses under pressure. Failure to do so may result in expending precious energy restoring unhealthy workplaces and relationships.

Since love is a highly emotional character quality, it must be guarded using wisdom and stewardship. An unhealthy amygdala could be easily reinforced by out-of-control emotions and/or activities. We must choose to love other people, which is best done with a healthy amygdala and by developing emotional stability.

Researcher and therapist John Gottman identifies five steps that help us develop positive emotional control. First, we must be aware of our emotions. In other words, we must recognize what different emotions feel like and learn to identify those feelings when we have them. This not only produces sensitivity to our own feelings but also increases our ability to identify emotions in other people. Second, we should recognize emotions as opportunities for intimacy and teaching. Parents or mentors can teach empathy and love by connecting with their child or mentee, recognizing the emotional challenges they are going through. They can create space to work through failed relationships, academic struggles, betrayal in friendships, spiritual challenges, or other negative experiences. Third, we must learn to demonstrate positive emotional feedback by listening empathetically and validating others' feelings. The validation process of empathic listening is vital for the development of emotional stability. Fourth, we must help people label their emotions as they occur. Providing words to help people define their feelings puts boundaries around the emotion and makes it a normal part of life. Fifth, we must have healthy limits around problem solving for others. The natural tendency for a mentor or parent is to solve a problem for the struggling child or mentee. However, the goal is to move the struggling person into a place where he or she not only recognizes the emotional tension but also develop his or her own problem-solving skills. Leaders give a great gift when they teach people to self-diagnose emotions and use problem-solving skills.[102]

Character Outcomes of the Fruit of Love

When we embody the fruit of love and master emotional stability, we will likely display several character outcomes. Four significant outcomes are forgiveness, courage, friendship, and reverence. First, we develop a posture of forgiveness toward others as we recognize the magnitude of the forgiveness Christ has lavished upon us. This recognition, coupled with emotional stability, allows us to forgive the wrongs committed against us. This involves not holding grudges and letting go of resentment to experience healing. Jesus powerfully displayed forgiveness by pardoning those who brutally tortured and crucified Him (Luke 23:34).

Second, we develop courage as an outcome of love, realizing that God gives us the strength to face difficult situations and trials. Courage is a confident response, knowing that God is in control and His indwelling Spirit is greater than anyone who might come against us. Joshua's relationship with Moses illustrated both love and emotional stability. When Moses passed the mantle of leadership to Joshua, he exhorted Joshua to have courage and strength in the Lord because God would be with him (Deut. 31:6).

Leadership transitions have emotional responses. Current leaders can hold on too tightly and not allow change to pass smoothly to the next generation. New leaders can move too quickly and make current leaders feel disrespected or overlooked. Transitions such as Moses transferring leadership to Joshua must be tempered with the kind of love that prefers the other person, communicating confidence that he or she will lead well, and filled with the courage to take up the leadership mantle.

Third, friendship develops as an outcome of love. Friendship involves companionship and closeness between us and others as we commit to forming and reinforcing character in one another. The wisdom of Solomon reminds us: "As iron sharpens iron, so one person sharpens another" (Prov. 27:17).

Fourth, the fruit of love is expressed through a reverent attitude, where we recognize and respect others not only because of their role or authority but also because they are created in God's image, regardless of ethnicity, gender, position, or personality. The apostle Peter offered some significant advice on how to live godly lives in a pagan society. He encouraged believers to submit to human authority for the sake of the Lord and to show proper respect to all people (1 Pet. 2:13–16). Peter's command to show proper respect to everyone indicates that all people should be treated as part of God's creation. People are to be respected in the same way that their Creator is respected. This can only be done with the help of the Holy Spirit, as He produces love in both our emotions and actions.

CHAPTER 13

Joy and a Positive Attitude

AS WE DEVELOP THE FRUIT OF JOY, WE BEGIN TO EXPERIENCE God's creation, His people, and circumstances with an attitude of acceptance, delight, and authentic happiness, while living in harmony with God and others. When we have embraced this attitude, we can maintain a joyful demeanor regardless of positive or negative circumstances or individuals. Jesus lived a joy-filled life despite circumstances. When He prayed for His disciples before His arrest, trial, and execution, He asked the Father to keep them safe and to fill them with His joy (John 17:12–13).

Leadership Quality: Positive Attitude

The second leadership quality developed in a person led by the Holy Spirit is a positive attitude. A positive attitude closely resembles joy. Paul David Tripp provides insight into the source of joy:

> I am more and more convinced that what gives ministry it's motivation, perseverance, humility, joy, tenderness, passion, and grace is the devotional life of the one doing ministry. When I daily admit how needy I am, daily meditate on the grace of the Lord Jesus Christ, and daily feed on the restorative wisdom of his word, I am propelled to share with others the grace that I am daily receiving at the hands of my Savior.[103]

This reflection is a reminder of the importance of personal devotions to our character formation. All too often, our leadership is not fueled by personal worship and intimate communication with the Holy Spirit but rather by guilt, performance, or the demands of our schedules. Combined with frequently feeling misunderstood or criticized by those to whom we are ministering, we can easily become entrapped by shame or the routine and mundane. The result of these misplaced motivations is burnout and a sense that ministry is no longer a privilege but rather a duty. Many leaders feel that they must grind out their ministry work just to get the job done. In the process, they lose their joy, passion, and personal worship life.[104]

A study conducted at Yale University School of Management found that cheerfulness spreads easily, while irritability hardly at all. The research showed that out of twelve hundred episodes of laughter in the workplace, the responding laugh came from a common statement such as, "Nice to meet you," rather than in response to a joke.[105] The conclusion is that laughter has immense connecting power between people. It creates a neurological reaction that interlocks limbic systems. People who enjoy each other's company laugh easily and often. Thus, we can conclude that everyone has the capacity to spread joy through shared laughter and a simple friendly greeting.[106]

Developing a Positive Attitude

Developing a positive attitude is fundamental to leadership. We typically develop our attitudes as we grow into adulthood, but with work and effort, we can also change and develop a positive attitude as adult.[107] Joseph Ciaccio provides seven tips to increase positivity in our leadership style:

First, seek solutions to frustrations. We must become aware of our internal emotional objections that inhibit us from addressing external problems. People often become negative about work conditions but cannot or do not tackle those circumstances because of a poor attitude. If we can learn to recognize our inner emotional state and try to change our feelings toward work, a solution to our external problem will most likely follow. Changing our internal emotions toward a situation generally helps us create a more positive experience for ourselves. When we begin to find external solutions, our internal emotions continue to develop in a positive direction, as the relationship between the two is reciprocal.[108] However, the solution starts with controlling our internal emotions.

Second, we learn to retrain our reactions. People are often pessimistic because that attitude has been modeled for them, but we can change that. Rethinking situations allows us to avoid reacting in an unhealthy manner. Thoughts control feelings and feelings impact our actions. Creating a list of positives about a seemingly negative situation can help us retrain our overall thinking patterns.[109] Along these lines, Reggie McNeal highlights the crucial role of gratitude in a leader's life:

> Gratitude focuses leaders on what they have rather than on what is missing. Gratitude taps into the eternal. The leader who practices gratitude gets a head start on heaven, because gratitude gives birth to praise, and giving praise is what we ultimately are designed to do. *A grateful leader has a heart of joy that is practically unassailable by bad circumstances.* This kind of leader proves particularly powerful.[110] (emphasis added)

grateful leader is one who turns the negative into the positive by thinking clearly about the best reaction to the given circumstances. In most cases, a positive response is the best response.

Third, we can create positive outcomes through positive actions. When we feel that our available options are limited, we often develop anxiety. When we actively research the scenario that is inducing our anxiousness and acquire more information regarding the situation, we create a greater possibility of finding a solution. Armed with these options, our positive emotions are likely to rise.[111]

Fourth, we can develop empathy. Understanding another person's point of view and adjusting to reflect that perspective helps us to develop a positive attitude toward situations and to lead toward a better understanding of the scenario. Providing clarity helps reduce negative feelings for everyone involved.[112]

Fifth, we can change our personal goals and objectives. For example, occupations such as teaching or ministry are often not well compensated. In a capitalist society, this reality is often viewed negatively. We run the risk of spending too much mental energy on this issue. Changing our goals or objectives to focus on the impact we can have on other people as opposed to concentrating on making a higher salary shifts our emotional state and bring satisfaction.[113]

Sixth, we can create a habit of prayer and exercise. Prayer routinely creates space to thank God for daily blessings. Praying through a list of our blessings reminds us of God's help and gifts to us, especially in tough times. Along with prayer, exercise physically releases tension, providing a place to channel counterproductive feelings and simultaneously creating a more positive attitude through the production of endorphins. Prayer and exercise can even be conducted at the same time.[114]

Seventh, we can get help from people worthy of respect. We ought to seek out people who have naturally positive tendencies and who are willing to give input on how to develop this attribute.[115] Leaders must intentionally develop a positive attitude to maintain a spirit of joy. A positive attitude has a lasting impact on people and improves the environment in which we work and live.

Character Outcomes of the Fruit of Joy

Gratitude and enthusiasm are two character outcomes of a positive attitude. Gratitude is an attitude of being thankful. Paul's final instructions to the church of Thessalonica encouraged them to have a spirit of gratitude (1 Thess. 5:15–18).

Enthusiasm, the second character outcome, helps us overcome disappointments and setbacks. It enables us to remain optimistic and zealous during difficulty. Ralph Waldo Emerson said, "Nothing great was ever achieved without enthusiasm."[116]

Scripture also encourages this idea of enthusiasm. Paul reminds believers to never lack zeal (Rom. 12:11) and encourages Christians not to become weary in doing good (Gal. 6:9). He encourages us to work with all our hearts, as if working directly for the Lord and not for man (Col. 3:23). Enthusiasm is an outstanding character outcome that is produced in us as we develop the fruit of joy and lead people with a positive attitude.

CHAPTER 14

Peace and Self-Assurance

THE THIRD FRUIT PRESENT IN A PERSON LED BY THE HOLY Spirit is peace. As we live a life of peace, we develop tranquility, completely surrendering control of our hearts, minds, souls, and wills to God.

Leadership Quality: Self-Assurance

When we are at peace with God, we have a sense of confidence, knowing that God is controlling the circumstances of our lives. Self-assurance arises from this peace. As we discover and fully embrace who we are in Christ, we begin to live self-assuredly.[117]

People often base their assurance on what other people think or on their successes and failures. These are problematic and inadequate standards. We must recognize that God has made us into new creatures through Christ's death and resurrection. He declares that His new creatures are righteous, loved, pleasing, and totally accepted by Him (2 Cor. 5:17–21, Gal. 2:20). Other people's opinions and the circumstances of life play a role in our story, but they cannot be the basis of godly self-assurance.[118] Thankfully, God never changes, so our assurance placed in Him is always secure.

When people believe in what God has done for them and accept who Christ declares them to be, it changes their behavior. The story of Zacchaeus demonstrates how Jesus's unconditional love and acceptance transforms us into different people. Zacchaeus radically altered the way he viewed himself, transforming from a swindling tax collector to a person loved by God. He repented of his sins and pledged to repay fourfold everyone from whom he had stolen. Through his relationship with Christ, he became confident, and his new-found purpose reshaped his behaviors (Luke 19:1–10).

Multiple factors can inhibit the development of self-assurance. Sometimes, parents and other authority figures in a child's life speak derogatory comments to the children in their care, not realizing how this harms their child's confidence. When parents criticize a child's behavior, manners, and mistakes to produce a better child, they inadvertently do the opposite. For example, parents might call their child hyperactive or lazy, thinking this will motivate the child to change his or her behavior. In fact, the opposite is true; mocking erodes a child's store of confidence.[119] Children respond best to positive affirmation in the context of a loving relationship.

The development of self-assurance can also be inhibited by lacking a sense of belonging reinforced by positive relationships. Belonging, an innate human desire, is so foundational that without it, we will settle for poor substitutes, such as giving in to peer pressure, getting involved in gangs, or gossiping. Brené Brown points out that "true belonging only happens when we present our authentic, imperfect selves to the world, our sense of belonging can never be greater than our level of self-acceptance."[120] To accept ourselves, we must first understand the importance of loving ourselves. Jesus's instruction to "love your neighbor as yourself," implies that we develop love for others by understanding God's love for us (Matt. 22:37–39).

Also, the development of self-assurance can be inhibited by shame. We often do not want to talk about things of which we are ashamed. Therefore, we bury shame in our hearts, only to have it manifest in destructive ways. Shame needs only three things to grow out of control: secrecy, silence, and judgment.[121] In such conditions, shame festers and develops until it becomes all-consuming. A person full of shame will lack self-assurance.[122]

Avoiding the causes of low self-assurance is crucial, but understanding ways to improve our self-assurance is also important. Ken Sayre has studied the use of neurolinguistic programming (NLP) to understand how language, both verbal and nonverbal, affects our minds.[123] With the use of NLP, Sayre pinpointed nine factors that build confidence: (1) experience: doing something repeatedly causes it to get easier over time, (2) perception: controlling how we perceive our experiences, whether positive or negative, (3) decisiveness: making quick decisions by trusting our inner voice, (4) empowerment: controlling our environment, emotions, beliefs, and actions without making excuses, (5) goals: setting goals makes us more competent and likely to make those goals happen, (6) action: knowing what we want to accomplish and putting a plan into action to get it done, (7) motivation: knowing what motivates us and putting it to use, (8) momentum: building and maintaining confidence, and (9) commitment: realizing what we want out of life and being willing to pay the price to make it happen.[124] Building self-assurance takes continual effort because, for most of us, it is not part of our natural DNA. Becoming at peace with ourselves means possessing assurance that circumstances and situations will work out because of our personal confidence that God's plan is for our ultimate good.

Character Outcomes of the Fruit of Peace

A self-assured person demonstrates three character outcomes: contentment, confidence, and wisdom. A content person is a person who is at peace with present circumstances and does not seek gratification or find happiness in shallow things. Paul exemplifies such contentment when he encourages the church at Philippi to be content in every situation, even while he himself is in prison (Phil. 4:10–13).

The second character outcome is confidence, which can look like assurance. When we exude confidence, we rely on God for everything in life and recognize that God is in control. Therefore, we recognize that we are not responsible for the results, only for being obedient. Paul not only expresses contentment in his imprisonment but also exemplifies confidence by declaring, "I can do all things through Christ who gives me strength" (Phil. 4:13).

Wisdom, the final character outcome, is demonstrated when we make high-quality judgments and decisions based on knowledge of God's Word and its application to our lives. David, a man of good judgment and wisdom, meditated on God's Word, allowing it to bring peace to his spirit. This gave him wisdom in dealing with his enemies and insight greater than his teachers (Ps. 119:97–98). When we seek Holy Spirit–driven peace, we develop self-assurance evidenced through character qualities of confidence, contentment, and wisdom—all of which are components of godly leadership.

CHAPTER 15

Patience and Grit

THE FOURTH FRUIT WE DEVELOP WHEN WE ARE LED BY THE Holy Spirit is patience. Being patient means demonstrating tolerance while facing difficult situations with courage and strength. Thus, a patient person controls his or her mind, which then controls behavioral choices, rather than allowing external influences to rule them. Jesus faced affliction as He stood on trial before Pontius Pilate. He was interrogated, accused, and jeered at by people, but He gave no response or reply to the charges (Matt. 27:14). The way Jesus endured His trial with patience demonstrates grit.

Leadership Quality: Grit

Grit, which develops through patience, is necessary for leadership in today's culture. James T. Bradford comments:

Do you have "bounce-back-ability," and can you cope with criticism? Unfortunately, leadership can be brutal. We are asking people to take on a role that will subject them to disappointment and, likely, personal criticism. Invariably they'll get hurt emotionally at some point. They may also face physical and spiritual exhaustion. The question is whether a leader has developed, at least at basic levels, the necessary coping skills to keep going.[125]

Our ability to deal with criticism or disappointment and not be emotionally hurt takes inner fortitude. Refusing to retaliate is counterintuitive. Without the restraint of tough-mindedness, many of us would react to instigation in an aggressive manner.

When we react to an external provocation with a show of power, the result is often loss of leadership influence. If we cannot lead out of humility, transparency, and trust, we often end up leading out of fear, self-protection, and control. Choosing to trust and be transparent is not normative for people in leadership. These decisions require mental commitment and controlled action.[126] Dan B. Allender makes an interesting observation:

This is a strange paradox of leading: to the degree you attempt to hide or disassemble your weaknesses, the more you will need to control those you lead, the more insecure you will become, and the more rigidity you will impose. It is a paradox because most of us have heard that we should lead by exerting authority, by "never letting them see us sweat." What we really need to do is to be human, while at the same time challenging others to become fully human themselves.[127]

When we employ an authoritarian leadership approach, we often lose our patience with others to gain control. Rather than addressing conflicts by fixing them together, we may impatiently single someone out as both the source of the problem and the one who must fix it—quickly. In some cases, this might be the correct action, but when we do it as a reaction rather than a measured response, we often involve a degree of heightened emotion that does not help the situation at hand. Congregational or organizational leaders may gain allegiance and loyalty through fear, but it is false devotion and will quickly dissipate as the leader's lack of humility and patience undermines the trust of his or her followers. Today, more than ever, young employees require trust from their leaders.[128] Learning to control our reactions and trust our colleagues is a true test of mental toughness.

Understanding the best process by which to motivate people is valuable in helping others develop grit. For example, parents often lack patience with their children and must learn not to push their children too hard. Harry Harlow and Edward Deci conducted a study to determine which rewards are most effective in motivating children: extrinsic or intrinsic. To produce proper behavior quickly, parents often use external reward systems. Harlow and Deci found that external rewards often yield a short-term outcome but are detrimental to long-term success. People are best motivated by internal or intrinsic rewards, such as relationships, purpose and meaning, or personal goals.

Understanding our own cultural context is an extremely important part of successfully influencing society. Our default response to cultural challenges can be to lead with authority, strength, and control. A leader with grit, or mental toughness, can moderate his or her actions to serve, influence, and make a lasting impact on the next generation. Victor Frankl, a survivor of the Nazi concentration camp Auschwitz, exemplified grit. Having studied under Sigmund Freud, Frankl viewed behavior from a deterministic mindset. However, he found a few individuals with grit in the camp who showed sacrificial love and shared their meager rations. In part, Frankl survived the horrible conditions because he found a deeper and more meaningful form of existence. Frankl quoted Friedrich Nietzsche to describe how he endured his plight: "He who has a why to live for can bear with almost any how."[129] In action, grit looks like practicing patience to serve others. Serving is what Christ came to do, and it is also what Christ compels His Spirit-led followers to do.

Character Outcomes of the Fruit of Patience

Humility, availability, and attentiveness are three character outcomes in a person demonstrating grit. Humility minimizes arrogance, removes pride, and tempers our natural tendency to think more highly of ourselves than others. Jesus, instructing His disciples, corrected their misconception of greatness, teaching that servants are the greatest of all. Even while teaching this great lesson, Jesus was serving His disciples by washing their feet (Luke 22:27).

The second character outcome, availability, focuses on being ready to adjust our plans and schedule to fit the desires of God and the needs of other people. It involves making our personal priorities secondary to the needs of others. Paul, upon receiving a God-given vision of a man in need of help in Macedonia, made himself avail-able, changing his plans and setting out to help him (Acts 16:10).

Third, grit-minded people demonstrate the character outcome of attentiveness, carefully listening to other people, showing respect, courtesy, and full concentration. Attentiveness also has to do with being unwavering and steadfast. Hebrews 2:1 encourages believers to pay careful attention to the truth to avoid drifting away. Life's challenges often test leadership capacity. Remaining steady through trials indicates strong, capable management and mental strength.

CHAPTER 16

Kindness and Empathy

KINDNESS, THE FIFTH FRUIT OF THE SPIRIT, INVOLVES A benevolent disposition and love toward people. When we demonstrate a spirit of kindness, we most likely also demonstrate the leadership quality of empathy, as they are closely related. While Jesus taught in the towns and synagogues, He also healed the sick and had compassion on the people because they were harassed and helpless. Jesus told the disciples that the harvest was plentiful but the workers few (Matt. 9:35–37). In other words, Jesus felt people's needs and urged His disciples to be involved in providing solutions.

Leadership Quality: Empathy

One of the deepest human needs is to be understood by another person. Empathy meets this need for humanity, and those who fully understand its significance have a greater capacity for leadership. Henry Cloud makes this observation: "We cannot grow if we are all alone emotionally. Life is too difficult. But if we know that someone truly understands, we know we are not alone with our feelings and thoughts, and we gain encouragement to persevere in our growth."[130] Everyone needs someone who understands their plight in life and authentically comes alongside them to offer support and comfort. For many people, the local church helps meet this emotional need.

The traditional definition of evangelism is to preach good news to the poor, but it must also include healing the broken-hearted, restoring sight to the blind, and setting the captive free, spiritually as well as physically (Luke 4:18). Tim Clinton notes that the church represents Christ to a world in desperate need of a loving, under-standing relationship:

> Until you understand your own capacity for foolishness and evil, your ability to care for and have compassion for others is extremely limited. Or put it this way: an awareness of your own evil thoughts, foolish attitudes, and subsequent behaviors leaves no room for self-righteousness and feelings of superiority toward others because of the compassion you develop for others in light of your own sinful nature.[131]

We can either embrace this lesson and empty ourselves to become the hands and feet of Jesus or we can be judgmental people who further hurt the wounded. The first scenario breathes life into the world, while the second scenario makes God weep and the world laugh at our hypocrisy.[132] Ultimately, an empathic leader views all of life's experiences as opportunities to grow and develop understanding about how to help others through difficulty.

Knowing the brain chemistry and physiology behind the expression of empathy is helpful. Our brains produce four essential chemicals, each serving a unique purpose. First, when we are faced with stress or fear, endorphins mask that pain and disguise it as pleasure. Simon Sinek declares: "You can't laugh and be afraid at the same time, laughing actually releases endorphins, which mask pain."[133]

Next, the neurotransmitter dopamine creates a sense of accomplishment and is responsible for the feeling of satisfaction we get after completing an important task. Dopamine can be highly addictive, and some of the behaviors that produce excessive dopamine can be harmful. Use of cocaine, nicotine, and alcohol all release dopamine into the system.

Finally, oxytocin and serotonin are connected to social interaction. When leaders create a culture that curbs social interaction, it also curbs the release of these chemicals, and employee satisfaction typically decreases. Ultimately, this sabotages the organization from within. Serotonin enhances feelings of pride, while oxytocin boosts confidence. Oxytocin is the most popular of the four chemicals because it also produces feelings of friendship, love, and trust. It is responsible for the feelings people experience when they are in the company of close friends or trusted colleagues.[134] Simon Sinek makes a powerful statement about the value of oxytocin:

> Oxytocin is not there just to make us feel good. It is vital to our survival instincts. Without oxytocin, we wouldn't want to perform acts of generosity. Without oxytocin there would be no empathy. Without oxytocin, we wouldn't be able to develop strong bonds of trust and friendship. Without oxytocin, we would have no partner to raise our children; in fact, we wouldn't even love our children.[135]

Creating opportunities for connections to develop and oxytocin levels to increase are vital for an organization and its people to have a sense of bondedness and empathy. To accomplish this, leaders must facilitate occasions for cooperative interaction and encourage security and trust. Loyal and committed followers emerge from this place of safety.

One of the great challenges in organizational leadership today is the lack of empathy. Smart executives run companies and manage systems, but there seems to be a lack of strong, empathetic leaders who connect with people. Bob Chapman, CEO of manufacturing technology company Barry-Wehmiller, states in Sinek's book *Leaders Eat Last:* "No one wakes up in the morning to go to work with the hope that someone will manage us. We wake up in the morning and go to work with the hope that someone will lead us."[136] Unfortunately, many leaders misuse their power and display narcissistic leadership with little to no empathy for those they lead.

Narcissistic leaders fake empathy, appearing to be supportive of people only for their own good. Such a leader is often still influential, appearing to be friendly and interested in others and playing the game of relationships well. Over time, this leader will monopolize conversations, directing everything toward themselves and their goals and becoming increasingly self-serving. When narcissistic leaders are not allowed to express themselves on their terms, they can become condescending and display sudden anger. Underneath these outbursts lies deep insecurity and inner battles of which they are unaware. The unfortunate outcome of this type of leadership is an organization with low trust and an unempathetic culture.[137] Sinek reflects on empathic organizational leadership: "Empathy is not something we offer to our customers or our employees from nine to five. Empathy is a second by second, minute by minute service that we owe to everyone if we want to call ourselves a leader. Leadership is not a license to do less; it is a responsibility to do more."[138] People know when a leader is being less than genuinely concerned or interested in their personal well-being. Spirit-led leaders have a keen sense of discernment and care for the people under their leadership.

Character Outcomes of the Fruit of Kindness

The leadership quality of empathy is connected to three character outcomes: fairness, generosity, and encouragement. Leaders who are fair seek to view situations from the perspective of all involved and to pursue the most equitable solution for everyone, even if it results in personal loss. Jesus taught fairness when He called His disciples to "do to others what you would have them do to you" (Matt. 7:12).

The second outcome, generosity, focuses on giving to others from the profusion of goodness that God has poured into our own lives. Jesus instructed His disciples to bless people out of the abundance they had already received (Matt. 10:8). This requires properly stewarding our resources and recognizing that everything belongs to God; we are simply caretakers of what He has entrusted to us.

The third outcome, encouragement, focuses on supporting and helping people as they walk through challenging circumstances. Paul encouraged the church in Thessalonica, and us today, not to be discouraged as the end draws near but rather to encourage one another and build each other up (1 Thess. 5:11–14).

The leadership quality of empathy, which is derived from the fruit of kindness, is an essential element in good personal and organizational leadership. Leaders who do not study this character quality will likely develop dysfunctional teams and struggle to lead their families, their organizations, and themselves.

CHAPTER 17

Goodness and Maturity

GOODNESS, THE SIXTH FRUIT OF THE SPIRIT, IS DOING THE right thing at the right time and is expressed as honesty and purity. As we mature, our motives are purified, and we focus on doing what is right in any given moment. Matthew 19:14–21 provides insight into the kind of maturity that leads to goodness. In this passage, the heart of a child is shown to be more mature and pure than that of a rich man.

Leadership Quality: Maturity

The leadership quality of maturity is integral to the development of the fruit of goodness, empowering us to respond to the needs of others above our own needs. Part of the maturation process is learning to let go of the past. We often do not let go of past experiences in our lives because we feel victimized by them. Instead of entrapping us, past experiences can provide insight into the cultural conditioning that established our frame of reference. In other words, we can gain good information from our past to create a better future. Reggie McNeal expresses this concept beautifully, saying, "Maturity comes when we can learn to appreciate how our hearts were formed, to look at our early cultural development as a gift. Sometimes these experiences and influences have been crippling or harmful. But God can turn the past that we find ugly and wish to expunge, into a beauty mark."[139] The process of maturity, therefore, requires us to recognize that the past plays a significant role in our personal development. In this way, difficult experiences can have a positive outcome. A. W. Tozer, says, "It is doubtful whether God can bless man greatly until He has hurt him deeply."[140] The thought of welcoming pain or discomfort is counterintuitive. Most people, even believers, can become angry with God at the thought of being hurt by Him. Considering that God allows pain contradicts how most people see God. Sharon Parks affirms: "If spirituality begins at the crossroads of awe and angst, human beings inevitably step into those moments when we are in awe of the vastness of the universe confounded by the agony of the innocent."[141] Navigating the maturing process is difficult under any circumstances, yet we must embrace the mystery rather than try to solve the puzzle. Each of us approaches maturity in a unique way. Therefore, while investing in the mature development of a mentee or child, mentors and parents should guide with flexibility and grace.

The neuropsychological dimension of maturity development is significant. Charles Golden, a neuropsychologist at Nova Southeastern University, established a five-stage theory of development. Each stage is the product of biological brain maturation and environmental experience. The first stage involves the lower brain structure, called the reticular system. Twelve months after conception (typically three months postpartum), a child has developed stimulation and responsiveness. If the reticular system is damaged at this time, the likely outcome is physical hyperactivity.

The second stage of development begins at the same time as the first stage and is also completed twelve months after conception. This involves the maturation of the cerebral cortex. Basic reflexes such as crying and grasping develop as this area of the brain grows.

The third stage also begins to develop along with the first two but continues until age five. Brain development at this stage involves learning how to differentiate between objects and how to concentrate. A preference for certain people, fear of strangers, coordination, crawling, and walking are all outcomes of this developmental phase.

The fourth stage occurs at the rear of the parietal lobe, which develops from about five to eight years of age. As this area grows, the child acquires understanding needed to learn to read, write, think logically, and use grammar. The preparation for formal education occurs as this area matures.

The fifth stage of brain development happens during adolescence when the prefrontal area develops. This area continues to mature throughout adolescence and is not completely developed until the mid- to late twenties. This area regulates planning and evaluation of behavior. Slow development or prefrontal damage might result in distractibility, mental inflexibility, apathy, hyperactivity, and lack of inhibition.[142] Understanding brain development sheds light on the false idea that individuals choose to be mature or immature. Maturity is a physiological process that each person must go through.

Parents and mentors of growing individuals must understand this developmental process. Kim John Payne describes three phases of parenting as children mature. The governor phase occurs in the first nine years. In this phase, a parent-governor provides clear leadership and sets kind but firm boundaries, providing an atmosphere of safety and health. The gardener phase occurs from nine to thirteen years of age. Patience and careful observation are necessary during this phase. Children need to experience parents who are listening, watching, and tuned in to the changes occurring in their lives. At the same time, parents must remain the leader and be responsible for final decisions. The guide phase occurs between the ages of thirteen to the late teens. During this phase, providing guidance through carefully communicating personal past experiences can be helpful. However, a helpful guide knows that there are many ways to process life experiences, and the young person they are guiding will likely have a few ideas of his or her own.[143] Jeffrey Arnett comments on emerging adult maturity:

> Learning to accept responsibility for yourself means taking over responsibilities that had previously been assumed by your parents and no longer expecting your parents to shoulder the responsibility for the consequences of things you have done. Making independent decisions means no longer having important decisions about your life made or influenced by your parents.[144]

During the guide phase, the parents' goal is to release their child into independence. Understanding the physiological and psychological components of maturation processes prepares parents and mentors to come alongside a developing child and leader and provide guidance along the way. Often, guides can feel discouraged by lack of results, but understanding the stages of development brings hope.

Character Outcomes of the Fruit of Goodness

A mature person will usually exhibit two primary character out-comes: honesty and purity. We are honest when we are forthcoming with other people and do what is right. This character trait allows us to earn trust because we are accurate with facts. Paul encouraged the Ephesians to be honest and speak truthfully (Eph. 4:25).

The second character outcome—purity—has to do with being set apart for God to use and involves becoming holy. When we are pure of heart, we do not allow negative influences to interrupt our growth in our personal relationship with Christ. Paul encouraged practicing things that are true, noble, right, pure, admirable, and lovely (Phil. 4:8). Putting these things into practice results in God's peace in us.

CHAPTER 18

Faithfulness and Team Orientation

THE SEVENTH FRUIT OF THE SPIRIT IS FAITHFULNESS, WHICH is faith connected to action. Jesus illustrates faithfulness in the parable of the bags of gold (Matt. 25:14–26). The master commended the two men who earned interest on the gold, but severely reprimanded the unfaithful servant who was paralyzed by fear and did nothing with his allotment. This servant did not take initiative, was not dependable, and was not diligent. He was not team-oriented in his approach. A key outcome of faithfulness is trust. Team members who act faithfully are people who can be trusted with greater responsibilities in the future. As in the story of the faithful servants, faithful people understand the overall mission of the team, take initiative to move the mission forward, and demonstrate the leadership quality of being team oriented. Team members can count on the dependability, diligence, and initiative of a faithful person.

Leadership Quality: Team Orientation

For people to work together as a team, they must develop trust. Patrick Lencioni provides insight into the kind of trust teams need:

> The kind of trust that is necessary to build a great team is what I call vulnerability-based trust. This is what happens when members get to a point where they are completely comfortable being transparent, honest ... where they say and genuinely mean things like "I messed up," "I need help," "Your idea is better than mine," ... [and] "I'm sorry."[145]

Team-oriented people trust each other and learn to be comfortable with being open, even exposed, to one another regarding their failures, weaknesses, and fears. Trust is based on the simple idea that when people are not afraid to admit the truth about themselves, they are less likely to engage in political behavior that wastes the valuable time of team members and accomplishes limited results.[146]

Team building is not just about getting better results or improving productivity; it is also about bringing people together in a mutually supportive and challenging environment to fully realize their potential. Good teams, led by good leaders, understand rhythms in work. They know when the team must pitch in and work hard together, and they also know when they can slow down and play. Team leaders develop an appreciation for the skills each member brings to the team and encourage all members to reach their full potential.[147] Max Du Pree believes a leader's skills are reflected in his or her followers: "The signs of outstanding leadership appear primarily among the followers. Are the followers reaching their potential? Are they learning? Serving? Do they achieve the required results? Do they change with grace? Manage conflict?"[148] Ultimately, the team leader is responsible for the potential of the team. Team leaders do not inflict pain upon their team but rather bear pain for their team. The measure of outstanding leadership is how well the team's collaborative efforts are producing measurable results.

If we desire to lead healthy and productive teams, we should understand the concept of participative management, as developed by Max Du Pree. In name, the concept sounds contradictory. In fact, participative management simply means that decisions are not arbitrary, secret, or closed off to questioning. Participative management is not a democracy. Having a say is different from having a vote.[149] However, collaborative leadership is powerful, and is both motivating and productive for teams.

Du Pree outlines five steps that help team members foster environments and work processes based on quality workplace relationships. First, we can show respect by understanding and appreciating each person's skills and gifts. Recognizing and embracing team members' skills develops trust. Second, we can create an environment in which beliefs drive policy and practice. A person's value system and worldview should be integrated into his or her work life, just as they are integrated into family life. Third, we can agree on the rights of work. Each person, no matter what role or position he or she is in, has the same rights. People have the right to be needed, to be involved, to have a covenantal relationship, to be held accountable, and to make a commitment. Fourth, we can understand the respective role and relationship of contractual agreements and covenants. Contractual relationships cover normal working expectations, while covenantal relationships entail hospitality and care in corporations toward the people who work for them. This includes welcoming employees' unique personalities and creative ideas when appropriate. Fifth, we can understand that relationships count more than structure. Structures do not have anything to do with trust. Trust is built through organic relationships, established as people work transparently together.[150]

Organizations led by team-oriented leaders have a "we" mentality as opposed to an "I" mentality. The hierarchal structure of most organizations often caters to an "I" focused mentality, wherein leaders use subordinates to implement personal agendas and often make them feel like hirelings rather than coworkers. Leaders who understand how to value, affirm, and use every member of the team see greater results in product development and organizational trust. Andy Stanley supports this concept: "The less you do, the more you accomplish. The less you do, the more you enable others to accomplish."[151] Most healthy employees are not afraid of getting involved and doing work. However, they want the feeling that their work has meaning and that they personally mean something to the greater good of the organization. Developing a "we" mentality does not necessarily mean that everyone always agrees. At times, leaders must make independent decisions based on confidential information or a big-picture view. In a "we" centered environment, people feel valued and can respect rare independent decisions because they are the exception rather than the rule.[152]

Character Outcomes of the Fruit of Faithfulness

There are three primary character outcomes in a person who is team-oriented: dependability, initiative, and diligence.

Dependability has to do with being reliable and trustworthy. When we are dependable people, we keep our commitments even if it means personal sacrifice. Paul speaks to this idea as he reflects on the true nature of being a disciple. Those who have been given this trust must prove themselves to be faithful, even at personal loss (1 Cor. 4:2). The second character outcome is initiative, which means taking the lead and recognizing what needs to be done before being asked to do it. Paul encouraged the church in Philippi to press on toward the goal to win the prize (Phil. 3:14). Acknowledging that we are not complete in our current state, there is more growth, maturity, and understanding that we should pursue. Take the initiative and run for the tape to become what Christ intended for you. The third outcome, diligence, is the characteristic of operating to the best of our ability with excitement and passion to complete quality work in a timely manner. Paul encouraged believers to work with all their hearts as unto the Lord (Col. 3:23).

Team-oriented leaders are faithful leaders to organizations and to team members. They know how to work hard, take initiative, be dependable, build trust, and appreciate the people with whom they work. Team-oriented leaders make organizations highly productive and have positive reports of employee satisfaction.

CHAPTER 19

Gentleness and Conscientiousness

THE EIGHTH FRUIT OF THE SPIRIT IS GENTLENESS. PEOPLE who demonstrate a gentle spirit are calm, self-aware, and tender toward others. They are also aware that their words and actions have either a positive or negative effect on people around them. Thus, when we have a gentle spirit, we will demonstrate caution and wisdom in interpersonal relationships. Conscientious people will also demonstrate the same restraint as gentle-spirited people, knowing that their actions affect those around them. Conscientious people are committed to getting the job done right and sticking with it until completion. They are careful, dedicated, often devout, and attentive to details.[153] Brent Roberts makes the following observation:

> Conscientiousness predicts health and longevity,
> occupational success, marital stability, academic

achievement, and even wealth. As a result, conscientiousness has become an important "non-cognitive" trait used in diverse fields such as economics, political science, and education.[154]

Conscientious people tend to treat other individuals with gentleness and care because they recognize the influence of their actions.

Leadership Quality: Conscientiousness

A conscientious leader demonstrates a gentle spirit in leadership, showing compassion, thoughtfulness, and discretion. A conscientious parent responds to his or her child's misbehavior with grace, aware of and understanding the precarious world in which children are growing up. When children go through difficult times, modeling conscientiousness helps them develop a sense of duty and follow-through. When navigating circumstances beyond his or her control, a child's greatest need is for a gentle, stable, and compassionate response from a conscientious parent. Kara Powell provides this parental encouragement:

> Don't panic! There are very few issues you will face as parents that are irredeemable, even the biggies. Regardless of the circumstances, becoming overly distraught or emotional, especially within earshot of your child, only heightens your child's sense of dread fear and shame … Don't fret or worry. Instead of worry, pray.[155]

Parents who use good judgment and wisdom know the value of teaching children self-control, constraint, delayed gratification, politeness, planning, orderliness, obeying the rules, and the importance of being a responsible member of society. Raising children to be conscientious and responsible citizens is critical to their future success, as Adrian Furnham asserts:

> We now know from longitudinal studies that adults who were low on conscientiousness in childhood achieved less in school, work and life, and endangered themselves and others by unhealthy, risky and even criminal activities. Such people have unstable relationships and end up poorer, sicker and sadder than average.[156]

Learning to control one's behavior early in life is a developmental skill that proves beneficial in years to come.

Adolescents with little to no self-control may engage in activities that have a negative neurological impact. Typically, such young people are not aware that their activities may cause chronic illness such as cardiovascular disease, diabetes, and eating disorders. Young people who learn to self-regulate and who can restrain aggression, selfish-ness, and impulsiveness are more likely to make friends and concentrate on studies. Parents and mentors who intentionally spend time monitoring, shaping, and modeling responsible, conscientious behavior offer young people a greater chance to develop these healthy character qualities.

Patrick L. Hill, a psychological researcher at the University of Illinois, published a study on the cognitive benefits of conscientiousness. He concluded that if a person has self-control and is organized (attributes of conscientiousness), his or her cognitive functions will withstand the effects of age and disease on the brain better than someone who lacks those qualities. Further studies concluded that people who are found to be conscientious as early as age eight tend to live longer. These findings can be attributed in part to the application of conscientious habits toward "health, lack of stress and avoidance of stressful situations, careful management of career choices, loyal friendships, a stable marriage, and other aspects of life that effect health and longevity."[157]

There are a few ways we can increase our conscientiousness. First, we can focus on specifics. Find small specific areas that you can improve, such as being on time to meetings. Second, we can make daily plans and stick to them. Making a schedule and following it encourages organization and self-discipline. Third, we can use reminders. If being conscientious does not come naturally, we may be easily distracted. Using sticky notes and phones alerts can be helpful tools. Fourth, stay social. Conscientiousness is a social characteristic. Staying connected to people who encourage conscientious behaviors such as being on time and developing a gentle spirit is helpful in developing our own conscientiousness.[158]

Character Outcomes of the Fruit of Gentleness

As we establish conscientious qualities, three character outcomes will likely emerge: compassion, thoughtfulness, and discretion. Compassion is the quality of feeling the pain and struggles of people. It helps us show love and concern, motivating us to meet the needs of others. A beautiful depiction of compassion is the image of a shepherd who cares for his or her flock, carrying lambs close to the heart (Isa. 40:11). Thoughtfulness involves considering the feelings of others before our own. Discretion keeps our minds focused on the task at hand and guides us in choosing words, attitudes, and actions carefully to avoid negative consequences. Paul told the Roman church to make every effort to promote peace and mutual edification (Rom. 14:19), which includes practicing discretion.

Conscientiousness develops personality character qualities that assist us in seeing the needs of people around us. A conscientious person demonstrates gentleness in leadership by recognizing the value of and seeing the potential in others. Conscientious people lead healthy lives, engaging in positive, meaningful activities with discretion.

CHAPTER 20

Self-Control and Discipline

SELF-CONTROL, THE NINTH FRUIT OF THE SPIRIT, INVOLVES discipline and restraint with respect to God and others. Paul captures the spirit of this fruit when he encourages believers to "hold on to what is good, reject every kind of evil" (1 Thess. 5:21b, 22). Personal restraint enables us to resist the temptation to engage in fleshly desires.

Leadership Quality: Discipline

Among the many character qualities that we can possess, discipline is one of the most popular ones to pursue in American society. However, many people express confusion regarding discipline and its practice. Discipline, or personal restraint, starts with delayed gratification. As Cloud and Townsend note: "We look for the 'quick fix.' We want what we want right now. We may want our pain to end, and our career to take off, or relationship to get better, but the clear teaching of the Bible, life, and all the research is that growth takes time."[159] Waiting for the good things in life is challenging, but discipline is more than just waiting. It includes making key decisions in advance with intentionality. If we hope for a good marriage, it is critical that we make appropriate relationship decisions. If we hope for good health, nutritious eating and regular exercise should be part of our routine. If we look forward to financial stability upon retirement, budgeting and financial planning must be a regular practice. If we hope for a vibrant spiritual life, it is necessary to engage in daily spiritual habits. Scott Peck describes the discipline of delayed gratification this way: "Delaying gratification is a process of scheduling the pain and pleasure of life in such a way as to enhance the pleasure by meeting and experiencing the pain first and getting it over with. It is the only decent way to live."[160] In order to attain the future results for which we hope, we must resist current urges that distract or detract from achieving those goals.

It is in the formative development process where essential leadership characteristics are developed. Starting the formation process early is critical to helping young people understand the benefits of lifelong discipline. Most parents, unfortunately, think that discipline is the same as punishment. Discipline is safe, corrective in nature, and is based on a model of learning. As a matter of fact, the word *discipline* comes from the Latin word *disciplina*, which means "to educate or instruct, to teach or to guide."[161] Discipline is a way of responding to behavior that provides guidance. When young people learn discipline through a coaching relationship, they are more likely to self-impose good discipline in their own lives as they become adults. Punishment is much different than discipline because it is not a safe response but rather a reactive response to behavior, intended to cause shame.[162] It is impossible to shame a person into better behavior because shame always produces a negative response, inflicting emotional and psychological damage.

Healthy parental or mentor relationships are key to a young person's maturity. When we experience hurt in relationships, we may have difficulty trusting God or other people. Consequently, building a lasting and respectful relationship is important for both the parent and the young person.[163] Quite often, strained parent-child relationships are a result of inconsistent discipline. The parent shifts from being overly generous to overly disciplinary. Trying to produce a desired response, he or she might offer incentives like treats or toys. When this proves ineffective, the parent may switch to aggressively demanding the desired behavior. As a result of this unpredictable relationship, a young person may develop a lack of trust in authority and miss out on the opportunity to learn self-discipline. Identifying this mistrust is relatively easy, but it takes a great deal of relational reversal to undo the damage it causes.

Discipline and creating disciplined people do not have guaranteed formulas. However, a few guidelines can help along the way. First, we should communicate clear guidelines to one another. The result of not receiving clear instruction is heightened tension and extreme misunderstanding. The best way to prevent sowing negative reactions in someone's life because of a misunderstanding is to start by giving clear instruction.[164]

The second step in this process is developing consistency; that's a grave challenge for this generation. Due to the inconsistency that they have experienced, young people have difficulty trusting people in leadership, whether in their homes, schools, churches, municipalities, or governments. As leaders of the family, parents must show young people what it means to be consistent.[165] If parents desire to produce people who engage in life with all its struggles, including spiritual battles and fleshly temptations, they must begin by identifying their own core values and living in congruence with their beliefs. In other words, parents should live out what they hope to produce in their children. This requires consistency rather than compromise.[166]

Third, parents must be reasonable. Sometimes, parents treat people outside their family with kindness, while treating their spouse or children unreasonably. Parents excuse this behavior because they see their strong actions as a means of creating a safe and reliable home environment. In reality, this dynamic is a fear-based form of discipline.[167] Young people who grow up in unreasonable environments typically experience emotional and/or verbal abuse and are prone to chronic anxiety, putting themselves down, and repetitive behaviors such as nail biting, hair twisting, cutting, and bed-wetting.[168]

The fourth focus for parents to keep in mind as they establish discipline is character-building. Too often, parents focus their attention and energy on external behaviors and neglect the invisible things that are growing in the heart. Self-discipline is a major part of establishing a life of character and integrity. If these qualities are developed in the heart during the formative years, they become the foundation for building a family legacy.[169] We will all be spoken of in a negative way at some point in our lives. People, events, evil schemes, and catastrophes can all discourage us, but these external and uncontrollable factors cannot take away our inner character. Character enables us to remain resilient during tough times; it has a "staying power" because people of character do not worry about their reputation, nor are they altered by circumstances.[170]

As parents build character in their young person, they must recognize the important role that *both* parents play in instilling this fundamental quality. While both members of the parenting relationship are important, 75 percent of children form strong foundational beliefs and core values when the father is present in the discipline process, as opposed to only 15 percent when the mother is the only parent imparting these qualities.[171]

Character Outcomes of the Fruit of Self-Control

As we learn to embrace self-control, three primary character out-comes arise: responsibility, efficiency, and obedience. Responsibility has to do with knowing and doing what is expected without being asked. Responsibility relies upon self-discipline. Choosing to engage in the right activities and stay away from the things that bring harm to us or others requires self-discipline. Paul indicates that God, the ultimately Judge, judges a person's actions (Rom. 14:12). Efficiency, the second outcome, refers to being well organized, competent, and resourceful. Efficient people make the most of every situation, seeking better ways to do routine tasks. The psalmist encourages people to keep track of each day to gain wisdom (Ps. 90:12). A disciplined person will not squander time but rather uses it wisely. The third outcome, obedience, focuses on submitting to God and other people in authority. Proverbs encourages obeying the commands of God that lead to a good life.

Conclusion

We have unpacked the leadership qualities produced by the fruit of the Holy Spirit. Initially, we develop these qualities as we engage in a growing relationship with the Holy Spirit. To grow, we must remain connected to Jesus, the true vine (John 15:5). Spiritual fruit and the development of leadership qualities emerge as we intentionally focus on our spiritual formation process. Every person, whether far from God or making disciples themselves, is in the process of spiritual formation. Since God created humanity in His own image, we possess the Spirit of God. As we acknowledge and welcome the Spirit, we begin the active process of participating with Him in forming the character qualities of God within ourselves, evidenced by spiritual fruit.

From the Spirit of God comes nine fruit. The previous chapters have demonstrated how nine leadership qualities connect to each individual fruit: emotional stability, positive attitude, self-assurance, tough-mindedness, empathy, maturity, team orientation, conscientiousness, and discipline. As we develop these nine qualities, it is likely that certain character outcomes will follow. We identified twenty-six character qualities typically exemplified by people growing in relationship with the Holy Spirit.

In order to embrace these leadership qualities and character outcomes fully, we must realize that this is a lifetime process, and we must enter into it with a personal commitment to engage with scripture, fellow believers, parents, mentors, teachers, and friends who will invest their knowledge and experience into our developmental process. Even with all this investment, some things can only be learned as the Holy Spirit speaks to our hearts. The Holy Spirit awaits the full commitment of believers who long to learn from Him and allow fruit to be produced in their lives.

Character Development Curriculum Overview

AS CURRENT MINISTERS RETIRE WITHIN THE NEXT DECADE and are replaced by this generation's young men and women, new leaders must understand that character is the foundational element of effective ministry leadership, and they must know how to develop it in themselves and others. To this end, I have created a character development curriculum and evaluation tools to help new leaders increase their understanding of the role the fruit of the Spirit plays in the process of developing their godly character.

Character development in young ministry leaders has become an urgent issue of our time, as students spend less time in formal ministry training. Biblical and theological education are imperative for ministry leadership, but leaders must also display a life of integrity and character for people to follow them to Christ.

I have developed eleven teaching segments to use with developing leaders. Curriculum sessions one and two lay a foundation for biblical growth, and the following nine sessions lay out a biblical understanding of the full work of the fruit of the Spirit in Galatians 5:22–23. The sessions connect each fruit of the spirit with its corresponding leadership qualities and character outcomes.

As you adapt this curriculum to your teaching setting, you might consider distributing a copy of your teaching notes with italicized words left blank to be filled in as participants follow along.

As you peruse the character development curriculum, keep in mind its potential to contribute to four areas of ministry leadership:

First, it contributes to the participants' biblical understanding of the fruit of the Spirit and the importance of allowing the Spirit to develop these character qualities in their lives. The Bible offers instruction regarding righteous living in many key passages. Paul charges Timothy to live righteously in 2 Timothy 3:10–16, and Jesus offers a great picture of what this looks like in the Beatitudes (Matt. 5:1–12). The virtues of righteous living that Paul suggests in Galatians are specifically connected to a source: the Holy Spirit. As participants choose to live a life connected to the vine of Christ and allow the Spirit of God to work in them, these biblical character qualities will become increasingly evident in their lives.

Second, this material helps spiritual leaders recognize the importance of the spiritual developmental process. A person experiences salvation when he or she accepts Christ. However, the development of faith happens over time. After a person accepts Christ, he or she must develop a personal, growing relationship with Him. This arises through the study of God's Word, prayer, meditation, and reflection. While this is established, so is relational growth with other believers, a growing awareness of the significance of corporate worship, and a missional desire to share their faith with other people.

Third, this curriculum contributes to the church by helping leaders understand the process of spiritual growth. Due to its ability to be replicated, church leaders can implement this training in various contexts. Without a thorough understanding of this process, many believers jump from accepting Christ to the congregational or missional steps of the Christian life without developing good personal devotional habits. This works for a time, but for individuals to fully engage in biblical growth, they must understand the spiritual formation process beginning with personal growth. This material provides a training program to develop Spirit-filled leaders in the church.

Fourth, this curriculum helps young leaders understand that effective leadership flows out of the work the Spirit is doing in their personal lives. Many current ministry leadership resources focus on leadership techniques, but these tools are most effective when leaders are engaged in a growing relationship with the Holy Spirit.

Finally, as leaders follow the Spirit and lead with character, Christlike outcomes become visible to other people. These outcomes not only affect organizational leadership but also affect a leader's daily life. In the end, God's kingdom will advance as church leaders recognize and put into practice the spiritual disciplines that are so vital to a vibrant and ongoing relationship with the Spirit.

CHAPTER 21

Character Development Curriculum

Session 1

The Formation Process: Legalism or Grace

1. Embracing the Spirit of God will produce fruit that has godlike character qualities.

    a. Jesus did not come to get rid of the law but to fulfill it. "I have not come to abolish the law, but to fulfill it" (Matt. 5:17–18).

    b. The law had become so complex that normal daily activity would offend it.

    c. When every action seems to be the wrong one, what do you do? Quit trying!

    d. It is likely that even the people who were *enforcing the law* were some of the worst offenders.

    e. Paul's message in Galatians is that *out of relationship* with God, we choose a better way to live. That relationship is developed by the work of the Holy Spirit, which Christ gave when He physically departed (John 14).

2. In Galatians, a scandal has broken out. One side feels *rules develop character* and the other side believes character *comes out of relationship*.

    a. Paul was clearly agitated by what was going on in the church he established.[172]

    b. The vision and values of this church had been altered from its original foundation. "I am astonished" (Gal. 1:6).

    c. "If anyone preaches something different, you are cursed" (Gal. 2:9).

        i. "Anyone." It doesn't matter who you are: sex, race, religion, or social status.[173]

        ii. God's grace should be the message.

    d. Key verse: "We know that a person is not justified *by the works* of the law, but *by faith in Jesus Christ.* So we, too, have put our faith in Jesus Christ that we may be justified by faith in Christ and not by the works of the law, because by the works of the law no one will be justified" (Gal. 2:16; emphasis added). Message: *no* to law; *yes* to grace.

3. God does not love us because of what we do but because of who we are.

    a. A painting on the wall: Can it become more beautiful by hanging on the wall? What would happen if you shined a light on the painting? When we allow *the light of the Spirit* to shine on our lives, the colors from the artist become more vivid. It's not the frame around the picture that makes the picture shine; it's the *light* that is cast upon its colors.

    b. When a person experiences the light of God's Spirit really shining on them, they will want *more light/ Spirit.*

    c. This light of God will produce *godlike fruit* which, makes a person's character more God like (Gal. 5:22–23).[174]

    d. What are common areas that could be viewed as legalism today? What about racial imperialism? Education? Cultural superiority? Morality? Religious superiority?[175]

4. The formation process must come from a personal desire to *know God and be with Him.*

    a. Personal: Choose a special time and place where you can meet with God.[176]

    b. Relational: Healthy relationships are to be honest and forthright, encouraging and loving.[177]

    c. Congregational: This experience is for us to corporately humble ourselves, not to be entertained.[178]

    d. Missional: The growth process must include the body of Christ. Without the body, the process is neither totally biblical nor orthodox.[179]

5. If a person doesn't grow intentionally, he or she will grow unintentionally.[180]

Session 2

Character Growth Is a Process

What does it mean when Jesus makes the statement, "If you love me, keep my commands. Because you love me and keep my commands, I will ask the Father (God), to give you another advocate to help you and be with you forever—The Spirit of truth" (John 14:15)?

1. What are the commands of Jesus? Love the Lord your God.

   a. Because you align your life with Christ, what will happen?
   b. Who is the Spirit of truth?
   c. Why is He the Spirit of truth?
   d. Later in the passage Jesus says people will struggle following the Spirit of truth. Why?
   e. It seems to be easier to *follow rules* because they are *visible*. Rules are not *faith or relationship dependent*.

2. Paul makes a similar statement in Galatians 2:20–21: "I have been crucified with Christ and I no longer live, but Christ lives in me. The life I now live in the body, I live by faith in the Son of God, who loved me and gave himself for me. I do not set aside the grace of God, for if righteousness could be gained through the law, Christ died for nothing!"

   a. Paul takes us back to the point of Christ's death. Why? *The Spirit is given.*
   b. What does Paul mean, "I no longer live, but Christ lives in me?"
   c. How does Christ live in us?

d. When a person fully embraces *the person of Jesus*, God's Spirit is evident in that person by his or her character. As a result, this individual becomes a relational change agent in the lives of others.[181]

3. Real fruit is produced in a person who is connected to the true vine. The Fruit Metaphor.

Jesus uses the fruit metaphor throughout scripture (Matt. 7:17–18, Luke 6:43–44). In John 15:1–12, Jesus says, "I am the true (*alethinos—real*) vine, and my Father is the gardener."[182]

a. The only way to produce real fruit is to stay connected to the real vine. Does a vine grow all kinds of different fruit? *No, one godly kind.*

b. Successful fruit growing is dependent upon *the skill of the gardener.*

c. What does a gardener do to help a garden grow well?

d. *(GK) Aireo*—To take away.[183] John 15:2—The farmer cuts off, prunes the vine. Why?

e. How does pruning influence us?

f. How does pruning influence God? Jeremiah 8:18–19:3: God weeps over the action He must take.

g. If pruning is a good thing for better fruit bearing, wouldn't it make sense that *we would welcome it*? Maybe even *self-impose it*? What does that look like? *Discipleship.*

h. Jesus identifies real believers as those who bear fruit, which represent *God the gardener*, in a positive way. The *character (fruit)*, developed in a disciple's life, is God-honoring (Matt. 7:20, Luke 6:43–44).

i. How does fruit grow? "I wait for the Lord, my whole being waits, and in his word I put my hope"[184] (Ps. 130:5–6).

j. As a result of good fruit bearing, we should start to *look the way the gardener designed us.*

k. Jesus said, "As the Father has loved me, so I have loved you. Remain in my love" (John 15:9).

l. *Love* is the key fruit mentioned in Galatians 5:22, and it is the first and greatest command.

Session 3

Love

The first character quality of the fruit of the Spirit is love. The central message of the Bible starts with God, who is love (1 John 4:8).

Christlike love is call *agape* love. It is self-giving, self-sacrificing—the type of love that Paul mentions in 1 Corinthians 13.[185]

Do the love test: Put your name in the place of the word "love" in 1 Corinthians 13.

1. Love Is Active

    a. Love, as a noun, does not appear in Greek writing, although it does appear multiple times as a verb.
    b. The Greeks referenced three other names for love: (1) *philia*, which is a warm, intimate friendship; (2) *eros*, which refers to physical love between sexes; and (3) *storge,* which relates to the love of family members. The references, which refer to God's love, always use the verb *agape*, which is the form Paul used in describing the kind of love we should also have toward one another.[186]

2. What does real love look like? 1 John 3:16: *Laying down one's life for another.*

    a. Love like this only grows with *intentionality.*

3. Love through *difficulty.*

4. How do we love people who hurt us, disagree with us, or make different life choices? *Stay connected to the vine.*

    a. Love covers a multitude of *sins* (1 Pet. 4:8).

    b. There is no fear in love; fear has to do with *punishment* (1 John 4:18).

        i. The martyr Stephen as an example. Fell to his death in Acts 7:60; his last breath asked the Lord to not hold the act of sin against his persecutors.

5. Love and Judgment?

    a. Today's culture uses the phrase, "Don't judge me."

    b. Paul tells us when we pass judgment on another, we *condemn* ourselves (Rom. 2:1).

6. How do we love people and not judge their actions?

    a. Who is the ultimate judge of actions? Including our own? God.

7. Love—Emotional Stability

    a. An emotionally stable leader can determine the *best response* to a situation.[187]

    b. *Emotional awareness/stability* is more important than IQ. It determines success in all walks of life.[188]

    c. The amygdala triggers emotion from the limbic brain structure. It can take over the rational center of the neocortex, which controls our fight, flee, or freeze in an emergency.

    d. Emotions will affect this area: jealousy, pride, contempt, fear, hypertension, pornography, stress, anxiety.[189]

8. Five Steps to Develop Positive Emotion[190]

    a. Be aware of emotion. Identify what it feels like.

    b. Recognize the emotion as an opportunity for teaching or learning.

    c. Listen and empathize.

    d. Label the emotion: "tense," "worried," "hurt," "angry."

    e. Provide limits to help solve the emotional problem. Some behavior is acceptable based on the season in life. Setting a limit helps a person know there will be consequences if I take this too far.

9. Character outcomes include

    a. Forgiveness.

    b. Courage.

    c. Friendship.

    d. Reverence.

Session 4

Joy

The second character quality is described as the fruit of joy. People will work a lifetime to obtain it but seem to never fully embrace true joy. True joy can only be obtained when a person is connected to the source—the vine, Jesus.

Paul used the word *chara* to describe this biblical expression of joy, which is unlike human happiness.[191] Paul encouraged believers to rejoice "in the Lord" (Phil. 3:1, 4:4; 2 Cor. 13:11). This joy, which comes through "faith," (Phil. 1:25) is given by God through the process of believing (Rom. 15:13). Its foundation comes through one's faith in God (Rom. 12:12) and originates from the Holy Spirit (Rom. 14:17). Paul calls joy a fruit of the Spirit because it was not subject to *human emotion* but a result of *divine inspiration*. Christian joy is not *circumstantial* but Spirit-inspired despite circumstances (2 Cor. 6:10, 8:2; 1 Thess. 1:6).[192]

1. Joy is counterintuitive.

   a. In Acts 5:41, the apostles rejoice after they have been beaten unjustifiably because of their belief.
   b. Joy came because of their disgrace for the sake of Christ.
   c. Joy is more than a happy countenance. Happiness is temporal based on circumstances.
   d. Joy is a deep response: I'm more mature (deeper) when my character is established through the Holy Spirit.
   e. Its presence is visible in good times but mostly present in difficult moments.[193]

2. Joy and Endurance

    a. In Luke 15:8–12, we read an example of what brings joy.

    b. After a woman loses a precious coin, she searches desperately to find the lost coin.

    c. After much searching, she finds it, and she rejoices.

    d. There are two parts to the story:

        i. First, the amount of *commitment* it takes to persevere to the end. The goal is joy but sometimes the circumstances we face require effort to work through.

        ii. Second, our mindsets must be positive and focused on the result. When the lost is found there will be overwhelming joy, so much so that even heaven will rejoice.

    e. We must remember, our circumstances build character. Biblical joy calls us to embrace our circumstances knowing the result is joy amid them.

3. Joy and a Positive Attitude

    a. The leadership quality of a positive attitude closely resembles joy.

    b. Paul David Tripp says, "I am more and more convinced that what gives Ministry it's motivation, perseverance, humility, joy, tenderness, passion, and grace is the devotional life of the one doing ministry."[194]

    c. This positive attitude enables a leader to work in difficult circumstances.

    d. Just before Jesus was arrested, He prayed for a full measure of joy in His disciples (John 17:12–13).

e. Study at Yale University: Laughter is more contagious than irritability or depression. Open loop circuits in the brain detect smiles and laughter and make people smile in return. Out of twelve hundred episodes of laughter, a responding laugh came from a simple "nice to meet you," not from a joke or sarcasm.[195]

4. Establishing Joy[196]

   a. Be aware of internal objection to your emotions, blocking responses to external problems.
   b. Change your thoughts toward or circumstance. Thoughts and feelings are controllable.
   c. Create positive thoughts that lead to positive actions. Do more research to find better results.
   d. Develop empathy. Understand another person's point of view to create a positive attitude.
   e. Change personal goals and objectives. Ministry is not well compensated; making money the focus will create negative feelings.
   f. Create a habit of prayer and exercise.
   g. Get help from people you respect.

5. Character Outcomes

   a. Gratitude.
   b. Enthusiasm.

Session 5

Peace

The third fruit of the Holy Spirit mentioned in Galatians 5:22 is peace. This character quality is not one that comes from a life without trials and troubles but rather is produced despite troubles and trials. The theme of peace is so prevalent in the New Testament that it is mentioned eighty times.[197] The Greek word for peace, *eirene*, is more than just wishing for goodwill and a life with no conflict. Peace is the idea of living in a state of wholeness.[198]

1. Peace and opposition.

   a. In John 14: 26–27, Jesus was troubled. He faced death in a manner that only comes when one has a calm confidence in God.
   b. In Philippians 4:11, while Paul was persecuted and faced prison, he wrote, "I have learned to be content *whatever the circumstances*" (emphasis added).
   c. Paul fully embraced hardship, knowing that the conditions could not change the *spirit* within him.
   d. When people allow the Holy Spirit to develop the character of peace in them, their circumstances will not determine their *attitude*.
   e. Peace does not come about through changing our circumstances but rather through a shift in our focus.

2. What focus should a person have to find true peace?

   a. Paul encouraged believers to let the peace of Christ rule in their hearts and the message of Christ to dwell among them (Col. 3:12–17).

b. As he preached to the church in Galatia, Paul's argument centered upon the inner work of Christ.[199]

3. Peace and Self-Assurance

   a. When a person's life is at peace with God and self, he or she gains a sense of confidence or self-assurance, knowing God is in control of the circumstances.[200]
   b. Lack of self-assurance often comes from focusing on what others think or on past experiences. Healthy confidence is built on the better foundation of what God says about His creation.[201]

4. Inhibiting Factors for Developing Self-Assurance[202]

   a. Derogatory comments spoken by parents over children.
      i. The use of negative labels (e.g., lazy, hyperactive).
   b. The lack of a sense of belonging through positive relationships.
      i. A sense of belonging is an innate human desire. People go to great lengths to belong to anything, positive or negative.
   c. Development of shame
      i. Shame grows in three ways: secrecy, silence, and judgment.

5. Ken Sayre offers nine factors that build confidence, using neurolinguistic programming (NLP), which focuses on how language affects our minds.[203]

   a. Experience. Doing something causes it to get easier over time.

     b. Perception. People can control how they perceive their experiences, whether positive or negative.

     c. Decisiveness. Making quick decisions by trusting your inner voice.

     d. Empowerment. People can control their environment, emotions, beliefs, and actions. People who are not empowered make excuses.

     e. Goals. People who set goals are more competent and likely to make those goals happen.

     f. Action. Knowing what you want to accomplish and putting a plan into action to get it done.

     g. Motivation. People are either motivated by pain or pleasure. Know what motivates you and put it to use.

     h. Momentum. When confidence starts to build, it is easier to maintain.

     i. Commitment. Realize what you want out of life and be willing to pay the price to make it happen.

6. Character Outcomes for Self-Assurance

     a. Contentment.

     b. Confidence.

     c. Wisdom.

Session 6

Patience

The Greek word for patience, *makrothymia*, is defined as "long-suffering."[204] When one has patience, one can control anger. When a patient person expresses anger, it is done under control. A patient person is one who does not get angered. Even when there is anger within, there is little expression toward others. Paul saw himself as a recipient of Christ's "perfect patience," so he could, in turn, be an example to those who would believe in God for eternal life. Paul referenced himself as the worst of sinners, recognizing that God, through His mercy, has been patient with him (1 Tim. 1:16).[205]

1. The Human Response

    a. The human response to an inanimate object that does not work, is a lack of patience.
    b. Biblical patience focuses on people. Biblical patience is described as long-suffering. Patience then it is to suffer long for those who would cause us distress.[206]
    c. In Romans 2:4, God shows his long-suffering for the arrogance of humanity.
    d. In what ways have you been tested to teach you to be patient with people?

2. A Bigger Plan

    a. When a person fully embraces Holy Spirit–guided patience, he or she will see life from a broader perspective.
    b. Too often we react impatiently to issues in life that do not go our way.

c. 2 Peter 3:9: God expresses patience toward people by referencing his patience with Noah.[207]

d. A broad perspective helps us to see that God is working out a bigger plan.

e. Proverbs reminds us that a hot-tempered person stirs up conflict, but a patient one calms a quarrel (Prov. 15:18).

f. Paul reminds us to be patient with everyone (1 Thess. 5:14).

g. A biblical model for Holy Spirit–driven patience is grace and mercy over anger and resentment.

h. What things can we do to help recognize God's bigger plan as he develops patience in our lives?

3. To Be Patient Is to Have Grit

a. Grit is when a patient person controls his or her mind, not allowing external influences to control his or her behavior.

b. Paul instructs us to be joyful in hope, patient in affliction, and faithful in prayer (Rom. 12:12).

c. Jesus was tough-minded and patient while he faced affliction during his trial (Matt. 27:14).

d. Do you have "bounce back ability," and can you cope with criticism?[208]

e. James Bradford said, "We are asking people to take on a role that will subject them to disappointment and, likely, personal criticism. Invariably they'll get hurt emotionally at some point. They may also face physical and spiritual exhaustion."

f. A study conducted by Harry Harlow indicated that *intrinsic* motivation is long-lasting as opposed to *extrinsic* motivation, which works quickly but has short-term results.

    i. Jessica Lahey said, "If you'd like your child to stop doing his schoolwork, pay him for good grades."[209]

    ii. Internal motivation over a long time creates results.

    iii. "He who has a why to live for can bear with almost any how."[210] This is from Nietzsche, following his survival in a Nazi concentration camp.

4. Three Character Outcomes from a Person Who Has Grit:

    a. Humility.
    b. Availability.
    c. Attentiveness.

Session 7

Kindness

The Greek word for kindness is *chrestotes* and means "goodness of heart." It can also be a reference to the generosity of God.[211] A person who allows the Spirit to lead him or her in this way is described as having virtues of gentleness, peacemaking, and getting along with people. Kindness does not infer that a person is weak, but it does mean that one has a good heart that resembles the heart of God.[212] Kindness is a quality of God that demonstrates that the fruit of the Spirit of God is active in a believer's life. The psalmist said to "taste and see that the Lord is good" (Ps. 34:8). God is kind, merciful, and gracious to His people. God is kind to the "ungrateful and the wicked" (Luke 6:35). Finally, Paul tells us that "God's kindness is designed to lead people to repentance" (Rom. 2:4).

1. Kindness with Purpose

   a. Luke 8:40: The woman who was sick with an issue of blood reached out and touched Jesus.

   b. Jesus responds to her: "Your *faith* has healed you" (Mark 5:34) (emphasis added).

   c. Biblical kindness does not just respond to human need to make someone's life better or happy. Biblical kindness goes beyond the immediate to the greater need: stronger faith. "God's kindness leads people to repentance."[213]

2. "A bruised Reed he will not break, the smoldering wick he will not snuff out" (Isaiah 42:3).

   a. The Assyrian practice was to crush anyone who was not loyal or displayed weakness.[214]

   b. The same was true for a smoldering wick. If it was only smoldering, it was seen as useless and tossed away.

   c. This is still true in our culture today as we see people climb corporate ladders of success.

   d. But a person with the character of the Spirit-led life sees *potential* in people. Jesus offers us a model of *grace* and second chances. Responding to a person who has done something wrong to us does not dismiss our *responsibility* to respond with kindness.

   e. Think of a person who has hurt you. What is the correct biblical response to this person?

3. The fruit of kindness leads to the character quality of empathy.

   a. One of the most significant human needs is to be understood by someone.

   b. We cannot grow if we are all alone emotionally. Life is too difficult. But if we know that someone understands, we know we are not alone with our feelings and thoughts, and we gain encouragement to persevere in our growth.[215]

   c. Empathic leaders will embrace every experience in life, realizing it is beneficial for someone.

4. The Brain and Empathy

   a. Four chemicals produced in the brain.[216]

     i. Endorphins mask physical pain; they are released in response to stress and fear.

     ii. Stephen Colbert said, "You can't laugh and be afraid at the same time, laughing releases endorphins which mask the pain."[217]

iii. Dopamine is released to make us feel good about a sense of accomplishment. Dopamine is highly addictive.

iv. Oxytocin is connected to our ability for social interaction; sense of trust, love, and friendship come from this.

v. Serotonin creates a feeling of pride and is released when a person perceives he or she is liked and respected. It is confidence boosting.

vi. Without oxytocin or serotonin being produced, empathy is not possible. Leaders who lead by *force* and *intimidation* lead with endorphins and dopamine, with a false sense of followership.

5. Empathy is connected to three character outcomes:

   a. Fairness.
   b. Generosity.
   c. Encouragement.

Session 8

Goodness

The Greek word for goodness is *agathosune*. It is a rare word that combines the doing and the being part of goodness.[218] Because it is strongly associated with the word *kindness*, it carries a similar meaning. The most common expression is found in the word *generosity*. Throughout Paul's writing in Galatians, "goodness" refers to God's faithful generosity toward those who trust His salvation found in Christ.[219]

1. Developing Goodness

    a. God's plan for His people is to *bear fruit* (John 15:8). He wants us to be actively doing good things.

    b. Jesus was a great example. He was filled with the Holy Spirit and went around doing good while healing people (Acts 10:38).

    c. God wants us to do good works, but our good works *do not save us*.

    d. We are saved by grace (Eph. 2:8).

    e. But a person who understands the grace given to them by God will also be a person who gladly fulfills God's command to do good works for others (2 John 1:6).

    f. Doing good *reflects the heart of God*.

2. Good to the *Hateful*

    a. One of the most difficult commands from God is to do good to those who hate you (Luke 6:27).

    b. People who are offensive and spiteful are not people we usually want to bless.

c. Jesus says, "It is no credit to you if you only do good to those who are good to you, even *sinners* love those who love them back" (Luke 6:32; emphasis added).

d. In what ways have you shown generosity to people who seem to be hateful?

3. The Fruit of Goodness Leads to the Character Quality of *Maturity*

a. Jesus blesses the children but cannot bless the rich man as he can't see the grip his vices have on his life (Matt. 19:14–21).

b. Past experiences develop maturity and produce a frame of reference for personal development.

c. A. W. Tozer, says: "It is doubtful whether God can bless man greatly until he has hurt him deeply."[220]

d. Reggie McNeal said, "Maturity comes when we can learn to *appreciate* how our hearts were formed and to look at our early cultural development as a *gift*. Sometimes these experiences and influences have been crippling or harmful, but God can turn the past that we find ugly and wish to expunge into a beauty mark."[221]

4. Maturity and *Neuropsychology*—Neuropsychologist Charles Golden (at Nova Southeastern University) Proposes a Five-Stage Theory of Development[222]

a. Each stage is the product of a *biological* brain maturation and *environmental* experience in five stages.

b. First stage: reticular system. Twelve months after conception. Stimulation and responsiveness develop. Damage could cause hyperactive behavior.

    c. Second stage: cerebral cortex, twelve months after conception. Basic reflexes such as crying and grasping occur.

    d. Third stage: begins at conception and continues to age five. Differentiation between objects and concentration; fear of strangers; preferences for people; coordination, crawling, and walking.

    e. Fourth stage: development at the rear of the parietal lobe. Develops between the age of five and eight. Preparation for formal education occurs. Reading, writing, grammar and logic develop.

    f. Fifth stage: development of prefrontal area of brain. Occurs during adolescence and is not completed until late twenties. Regulating the planning and evaluation of behavior.

5. Two primary character outcomes occur through maturity:

    a. Honesty.
    b. Purity.

Session 9

Faithfulness

A faithful person can be characterized by the words *trustworthy* and *reliable*. The Greek word is *pistis*, which indicates the type of person in whom one has complete confidence. You can put your faith in a person who is trustworthy and reliable. A person who demonstrates the characteristic of biblical faithfulness is a person who can be relied upon and trusted.[223]

1. God is faithful.

   a. "When we are *faithless*, He remains *faithful*, for He cannot disown himself. God's nature embodies the character quality of faithfulness" (2 Tim. 2:13).
   b. Paul writes, "Can the unfaithfulness of God's people nullify the faithfulness of God?" (Rom. 3:3). The answer is no, even though we are not faithful, God still is.[224]

2. Abraham was faithful.

   a. Abraham was called God's friend because God could count on him.
   b. Abraham was passionate about what God called him to do even though he *did not understand it* (James 2:23).
   c. Abraham was faithful (*pistis*) and the Lord saw him as righteous (Gen. 22).
   d. "Abraham believed God, and God saw him as righteous" (Gal. 3:6).[225]
   e. Faithfulness will grow as a person invests in his or her relationship with God. A person who is new to

faith does not have much faith; therefore, he or she is not viewed as faithful. As a person experiences the faithfulness of God, faith grows. As faith grows, so will faithfulness.

    f. What has God used in your life to make your faith grow?

3. The fruit of faithfulness produces the leadership quality team orientation.

    a. A biblical example: the master who entrusted three servants with bags of gold. Two improved the team and were placed in charge of more. One looked out for himself and was considered lazy (Matt. 25:14–26).

    b. Trust is at the root of team.

        i. Patrick Lencioni said, "The kind of trust that is necessary to build a great team is what I call *vulnerability-based* trust. This is what happens when members get to a point where they are completely comfortable being transparent."[226]

    c. Team leaders understand the importance of rhythm. Went to work to play. Rhythm helps establish team potential.[227]

4. Teams and Participative Management—Max Depree.[228]

    a. Everyone is involved in decisions. Having a say is different from having a vote.

    b. Five steps which helps team members foster relationships:

        i. Respect people. Have an appreciation for each individual's skill and gift.

ii. What we believe precedes policy and practice. A person's value system should be integrated into his or her work life.
iii. Each person has the same rights. Right to be needed, be involved, have a covenantal relationship, and to be accountable.
iv. Understand and respect the role and relationship of contractual and covenant agreements.
v. Understand that relationships count more than structure.

c. Organizations let by team-oriented leaders have a "we" mentality as opposed to an "I" mentality.
i. Andy Stanley said, "The less you do, the more you accomplish. The less you do, the more you enable others to accomplish."[229]

5. Three Character Outcomes of a Team-Oriented Leader

a. Dependability.
b. Initiative.
c. Diligence.

Session 10

Gentleness

Gentleness is a fruit of the Spirit that is essential in building and maintaining relationships. In our current culture, we are encouraged to "say what we think." I have heard comments from spiritual leaders regarding the use of adult language as being normal. Those who cannot handle this language are not living in the "real world." When a person displays the character quality of gentleness, a person has an even temper, an unpretentious attitude, and his or her passions are under control. Gentleness comes from the Greek word *praos,* which means meekness and humility.[230] The spirit of gentleness should never be misunderstood to mean weakness, as it relates to a person who has meekness or humility. It takes strength to be an individual of gentleness—the strength of God's Spirit.

1. The Lowly Yoke

    a. Matthew 11:29: In Matthew, God is revealed through Jesus in a prayer. Jesus is referencing His father's words as He instructs a person to "take my yoke upon you."
    b. The reference of the yoke is a reference to low stature.
    c. The lowest of people groups would use a yoke to pull heavy loads.
    d. To fully understand this, the yoke is about slavery or total submission to the master.
    e. God is not imposing slavery upon us, but rather suggesting that, as a person of the Spirit, we would impose upon ourselves.
    f. Jesus implies if a person would submit to a low position of gentleness, there he or she would find rest for the soul.[231]

2. The Gentleness of Christ

   a. Paul makes a statement about the gentle character of Christ when he appeals to the church in Corinth. He says, "By the humility and gentleness of Christ, I appeal to you" (2 Cor. 10:1).
   b. Paul's reputation was not one of gentleness. Quite the opposite!
   c. But when Paul was physically present with people, with the help of the Spirit of God, he would demonstrate a more timid demeanor—a demeanor that resembled Christ.[232]
   d. Paul again references Christ's character where he says, "In your relationships with one another have the same mindset as Christ" (Phil. 2:5). He is referencing the quality of a humble character that Jesus possessed.
   e. When you think of the word *gentle*, who comes to mind that resembles this character quality? Why?

3. The fruit of gentleness leads to the leadership quality of being conscientious.

   a. Paul instructs Timothy to make a conscientious effort to act rightly in his leadership. Timothy displays gentleness in his leadership choices (2 Tim. 2:22–24).
   b. Brent Roberts said, "Conscientiousness predicts health and longevity, occupational success, marital stability, academic achievement, and even wealth."[233]
   c. Children who have been raised by conscientious parents and grow up as conscientious adults make greater contributions to society and are likely to be more successful.

    d. Adrian Furnham said, "Studies show that adults who were low on conscientiousness in childhood achieved less in school, work, and life, and endangered themselves and others by unhealthy, risky and even criminal activities. Such people have unstable relationships and end up poorer, sicker, and sadder than average."[234]

    e. Studies indicate the benefits of being conscientious: age, less disease, longer life, lack of stress, better career choices, friends, marriage.[235]

    f. How to increase conscientiousness:

        i. Focus on specifics, for example being on time.

        ii. Make daily plans and stick to them. Encourages self-discipline.

        iii. Use reminders cell phone apps or sticky notes.

        iv. Stay social. People can encourage this behavior if you hang out with the right people.[236]

4. Character outcomes include

    a. Compassion.

    b. Thoughtfulness.

    c. Discretion.

Session 11

Self-control

The word *self-control* comes from the word *enkrateia*. The word has two parts, *en* means in, *krateia* means "power." Together, self-control means "in power." The term does not appear many times throughout scripture in the same context as it does in Galatians 5. However, it is mentioned more in the New Testament than in the Old Testament.[237]

In Acts 24:2, 5 Paul is on trial for causing trouble. The only "trouble" he caused was his announcement of what will happen to the resurrection of the dead. When the governor, Felix, visits Paul while in prison, Paul talks to him about righteous living and self-control (*enkrateia*). Felix becomes afraid and leaves Paul in jail for two more years.[238]

Titus 1:8 provides an outline of the character qualities required in a person who is selected as an overseer or elder. This person must demonstrate mature character. Paul states that such a person should be self-controlled, upright, holy, and disciplined.

1. Who is in control?

    a. Since self-control refers to power, it is important to ask the question, "Who is in power? Who are people of influence? Are we personally in power? Is God?

    b. God must be in power for one to have the character quality of self-control that God intends for those of Christian character and leadership to have.

    c. God's Spirit is in control to help us overcome the temptations that we face.

2. The opposite of self-control is self-indulgence.

   a. Matthew 23:25: Matthew uses strong language as he addresses those in leadership viewed as hypocritical. These leaders give off a persona of cleanliness, but they are full of greed and self-indulgence.
   b. The Greek word *akrasi* means "being without self-control."[239]
   c. Paul speaks to this issue when he advises unmarried people who lack self-control to get married. However, he would rather a person of biblical character use God-empowered self-control (1 Cor. 7:9).

3. What are areas in a believer's life that lack self-control?

   a. Self-control and the mind
   b. Proverbs 4:23 gives wise advice to guard one's heart, for it is the wellspring of life. Here, "heart" is referencing the *mind* and all that comes from it.
   c. When one sins, he or she sins twice: first in the mind and then in actions.
   d. The development of self-control must start with the mind. We must keep it centered on who God is.
   e. How can a spiritual formation strategy help guard our mind? Reiterate the growth strategy.

4. The fruit of self-control develops the leadership quality of discipline.

   a. Discipline, or personal restraint, is required to resist evil or fleshly desires (1 Thess. 5:21b, 22).
   b. Discipline helps us understand delayed gratification.

    i. Henry Cloud said, "We look for the 'quick fix.' We want what we want right now. We may want our pain to end, our career to take off, or relationships to get better, but the clear teaching of the Bible and secular research indicates that growth takes time."[240]

    ii. Delayed gratification is making key decisions in advance with intentionality. If you want a good marriage, make good dating decisions. The same applies to financial stability, health, spiritual life, disciplined children, etc.

    iii. Scott Peck said, "Delaying gratification is a process of scheduling the pain and pleasure of life in such a way as to enhance the pleasure by meeting and experiencing the pain first and getting it over with. It is the only decent way to live."[241]

    iv. The word *discipline* comes from the Latin *disciplina*, which means to educate or instruct, teach, or guide.

c. Steps to Discipline[242]

    i. Give clear instructions. People should know what is expected.

    ii. Be consistent. Living by core values builds trust. People today need congruent leadership for trust to be established; otherwise, they might quit in the process.

    iii. Be reasonable. Healthy communication, active listening, refusal to overreact to situations, and avoidance of negative body language are critical.

iv. Be a person of character. External behavior is often the primary focus, while what grows in the heart is not visible. Be careful who you talk about and how you use your words. Character will help a person remain resilient.

v. Believe in people. Most people struggle with low self-esteem from being put down by peers/parents. People need life-giving words.

5. Three Primary Character Outcomes of Self-Discipline

    a. Responsibility.
    b. Efficiency.
    c. Obedience.

CHAPTER 22

Character Development Evaluation Tools

SHOULD YOU CHOOSE TO EVALUATE YOUR BIBLICAL CHARACTER teaching sessions to determine their effectiveness in achieving your learning outcomes, you may choose to adapt the following character development survey for your purposes. You can utilize it as a pretest-posttest instrument to compare student answers prior to the teachings and after the final teaching. This will provide a framework to help them think about how they are developing character qualities while responding to life issues. Participants answer identical questions in the pretest and posttest as a means of determining whether the teaching brought about a statistically significant transformation in their lives.

You may wish to reassure students of the anonymity of the instrument and protect their privacy. In working with this new generation of leaders, I have learned that trust is especially important. Some instructors attach a number to each student's pretest-posttest to compare the pretest results to the posttest results while maintaining a measure of anonymity. You will need to determine what works best for your setting. Some people may feel that a survey connected to a number could reveal their identities, and that may keep them from being completely honest or from giving an authentic response.

Character Development Survey

Please select one choice.

Question	Strongly Disagree	Disagree	Neither Agree nor Disagree	Agree	Strongly Agree
1. I feel content with the amount of time I spend on spiritual growth.					
2. I am committed to the time and energy it takes to develop character in my life.					
3. I consistently follow a plan for spiritual growth.					
4. I am motivated to do for others what Christ has done for me, without qualification or reciprocation.					
5. When faced with challenging circumstances, I keep my emotions under control.					
6. I experience joy on a regular basis and my happiness is not dependent upon my current situation.					

7. Difficult circumstances and/or people affect my attitude in a negative way.					
8. I find myself fatigued by the turmoil in my life.					
9. I have an absence of inner peace.					
10. I have allowed circumstances and/or relationships to affect my self-confidence.					
11. I am easily aggravated when things go wrong or when people irritate me.					
12. I work to maintain a healthy mental attitude while experiencing difficult circumstances.					
13. It is my goal to serve people with kindness, focusing on the needs of others over my own personal needs.					
14. I show sympathy when I sense emotional tension.					
15. My life reflects the goodness of God, and I desire to see others experience God in their own lives.					
16. I struggle with indifference toward certain groups of people.					
17. I work to include people in decisions and activities despite personality or socioeconomic differences.					

18. I do not come across as harsh or headstrong in my interactions with others.					
19. I am a team player, collaborating with people to generate successful goals and constructive outcomes.					
20. I allow the Holy Spirit to direct me toward the things that please God and help me serve people.					
21. I seek to control my actions to do what is right.					
22. I welcome correction, whether self-imposed or from external sources.					
23. The teaching sessions helped me grow in my leadership role.					
24. The content of the teaching sessions was good.					

Open-Ended Questions

Using the above Likert Scale response device provides the best option for acquiring quantitative data. However, you can augment that feedback with questions such as the following and attach them to the end of the posttest survey to determine effectiveness of your delivery and whether the participants felt the material was beneficial.

Q25. The teaching sessions helped me grow in my leadership role.

Q26. The content of the teaching sessions was good.

Short Reflection Paper

As another aspect of evaluating your teaching, you may also wish to have participants write a short reflection paper to identify two items that stood out to them from the teaching sessions. Highlights from a few of the responses I received are listed below:

1. Rather than viewing the fruit [of the Spirit] as a self-help guide to being a "better person," infant Christians would realize that their power source is someone so much more trustworthy than themselves and that they can live in so much freedom by attuning their hearts to His.

2. I've been personally affected by Phil's work. It is not only helping the ministries that I serve but it is helping me personally. The heart behind the work is what makes it more beautiful. Young people want to be more like Jesus, but they do not know what that would look like let alone what structures and habits need to be in place to make that happen. Phil's work is making that possible. For that it should be read, commended, and, most importantly, put into practice.

3. This is not only the best explanation of leadership identification I have ever seen but beyond that, it is one of the greatest identification tools for authentic Christian living I have ever seen. I am a psychology major, but my dream is to go into youth and young adult leadership within the church. Getting the opportunity to be a part of the class was such an amazing opportunity. One thing I think is critical to note is the concept of spiritual disciplines, which are religious, and leadership qualities, which are cultural, and pairing them with psychological studies and ideas, which are innately scientific, gives these

concepts another element of stability and importance that is rarely seen in any such conversations today.

4. Pastor Phil managed to bring a brand-new perspective to the fruit of the Spirit, a verse I have read and said a thousand times in my childhood. The idea of spiritual development was not something I ever saw as something to study or something to focus on. I had never emphasized its importance—that was until he started to share his thoughts and research. There are few things more important to our relationships with Jesus. This study is a comprehendible, applicable way of learning to love, look, and live more in alignment with that of Jesus.

Conclusion

I have provided both teaching and assessment resources for training young ministry leaders in character development. The process of leading a life of character made effective by the empowerment of the Spirit requires commitment and dedication. It begins when we understand that we must remain connected to the vine of Christ (John 15:5) as the source of Spirit-inspired leadership. This process includes intentionally embracing formational development through meditation upon the Word, a relationship with the Spirit that produces godly fruit, and a personal awareness of character qualities, which produce twenty-six outcomes for maximum kingdom leadership. Leaders who embrace this character growth process will not only lead effectively but will also reflect the Spirit of God in a respectable way, giving glory to Him through their actions and outcomes.

CHAPTER 23

Final Thoughts

Implications of This Project

ONE OF THE MOST SIGNIFICANT IMPLICATIONS OF RESEARCHING this book has been the realization that leaders are not fully grasping scripture. While that is a broad statement, I believe it accurately represents the reality of most new leaders today. Participants involved in my initial project could be considered some of the best and brightest new leaders. Yet prior to the teaching sessions, some of them admitted to not having a basic understanding of the role the Holy Spirit plays in a person's life. Perhaps current church leaders assume that people understand the work of the Spirit due to the Pentecostal heritage of the church or from the person simply attending a Pentecostal church. Unfortunately, many churches are not teaching believers about the role of the Holy Spirit in a way that connects with new leaders. Other churches have completely abandoned teachings on the Holy Spirit due to the potential of theological controversy.

Another outcome of my research has been gaining clarity regarding the connection between psychological processing and spiritual engagement. While doing research and teaching this material, I found a profound connection between the way people think and the way they process their spiritual lives. Jesus, quoting the *Shema* (from Deut. 6:4), appropriately connects all the parts of the body when He calls believers to "love the Lord God with your heart, soul, strength, and mind" (Luke 10:27). Compartmentalizing the various aspects of our lives is not an optimal approach. On the contrary, we should see life as an interconnected whole. I was affirmed in this by the psychology major student who participated in my own teaching of this curriculum, who grasped this concept clearly and saw it as a new idea for her faith development.

Leadership theory, which is studied by many people from a variety of walks of life, has powerful biblical roots that influence daily life. It is not enough to know these roots; we must live them out. Unfortunately, there is a divide between knowing and doing, and church leaders must bridge that divide in the minds of developing leaders.

Recommendations for Growing Leaders

My first recommendation for growing leaders focuses on anyone who wants a growing and productive spiritual life. The need for personal spiritual growth cannot be overemphasized since spiritual growth only comes as we commit our time toward this effort. Personal and spiritual development must be scheduled like any other priority. Scheduling time with the Lord will ensure that nothing interferes or gets in the way of this important event happening daily. Personal growth requires intentionality. Paul called leaders to work on spiritual development purposefully (Phil. 2:12b–13). Budgeting time involves examining the priorities of our hearts. Jesus spoke about the priorities of life, and He connected the heart with what we treasure (Matt. 6:21). A spiritually vibrant and growing relationship with God requires a daily commitment of time.

For the past thirty-five years, I have focused on student spiritual formation. While growing churches engage in the culture to stay relevant, they must balance youth programs and events with in-depth biblical training. To accomplish this goal, leaders must model Christlike behavior and develop relationships with students. From that relationship, they can grow a healthy discipleship program. While this discipleship program may have less participation than other events, it should be seen as normative and necessary in the scope of the overall ministry structure. Even Jesus had only twelve disciples in His inner circle, three of whom were especially close to Him.

Christian universities could benefit from implementing a character development seminar or class. Due to their nature as educational institutions, Christian university settings provide a conducive environment for such programs, which go hand in hand with the mission focus of educating learners. Young people who come to a Christian university come with the inherent purpose of learning Christian ideals with increased rigor and are ready and willing for this kind of training.

To produce more Spirit-filled leaders with biblically based leadership qualities, it is imperative that new leaders receive quality teaching that enables them to engage in the process with enthusiasm and open hearts and minds. My research for this book was enhanced by quality resources used for development of the biblical-theological underpinnings and the resources regarding leadership.

One resource that greatly influenced me was *Primal Leadership* by Daniel Goleman, Richard Boyatzis, and Annie McKee. Together, the authors analyzed five hundred global companies including health care providers, academic institutions, government agencies, and religious organizations to determine which personal capabilities produced outstanding performance within the organizations. This resource offered insight on many pertinent issues related to human behavior, the function of the brain within the context of behavior, and its impact on leadership. As I looked through the lens of the fruit of the Spirit, the most applicable area for this book's content related to the leadership ability to love others as Christ loves them.

Another landmark book is by Joseph Ciaccio, who taught history for thirty-one years in a middle school on Long Island, New York. His years of experience led him to believe that many students and teachers do not fit into the traditional school system. He developed his own approach to teaching, which focuses on a more positive approach, hence the name of his book: *Totally Positive Teaching*. Ciaccio's book offers five methodologies whereby students become more self-disciplined, and underachievers become self-motivated. Generating character in future leaders requires an understanding of what motivates current learners as well as an understanding of effective approaches to teaching. The notion of developing character in an individual is culturally counterintuitive, especially when that character originates from the Holy Spirit.

Leaders Eat Last by Simon Sinek is inspirational for developing teams and understanding organizational behavior. The thesis in this book is not to produce new ideas on leadership but rather to create a generation of leaders who understand that the world will not be changed through mere managerial acumen but through leadership excellence. Sinek uses the military as the primary example of excellent leadership. Great leaders care about the people they are privileged to lead, and they understand that leadership is an honor that has a cost and comes at the expense of self-interest. Sinek's first work, *Start with Why*, influenced me early in my own leadership development, as he focuses on current culture and how to inspire people to action.

These resources and the others utilized for this book provided a bedrock understanding of the fruit of the Spirit and how a growing relationship with Jesus is imperative for true leadership character development.

Conclusion

I N AN ERA WHEN THE CHURCH IN AMERICA IS FACING DECLINE and even death due to the lack of competent leadership, this book seeks to reassert the need to develop leaders who understand who the Holy Spirit is and to develop character by embracing what the Spirit does in their lives. The erosion of the moral fabric in American society is seeping into the church and Christian homes because of shallow biblical understanding. We need quality Spirit-filled leadership who train believers to be parents who model a Christ-centered life, so that their children may begin lives of godly character at an early age under the leadership of the Holy Spirit. Unfortunately, for many people, faith is relegated to the hour spent in church on Sunday morning and never integrated into the workplace, where unsaved people need a witness of God's transforming power, or the home, where children need their parents to be models of godly character.

We need a biblical understanding of godly character and the empowerment of the Holy Spirit, who enables believers to implement these qualities into their daily lives. For Christians to be Christlike, they must possess the Spirit of Christ—the Holy Spirit—who causes the growth of the fruit of the Spirit and gives believers the ability to lead with powerful effectiveness.

A Spirit-filled leader will demonstrate character outcomes that other people can easily identify. The twenty-six outcomes discussed in this book are some of the possibilities. Jesus taught that He is the vine, and His followers are the branches. If we stay connected to the vine, we will produce spiritual fruit (John 15:5) as evidenced by love, joy, peace, patience, kindness, goodness, faithfulness, gentleness, and self-control. The fruit of the Spirit can look like many characteristics, but it should always resemble and point to the vine, Jesus Christ.

ENDNOTES

Chapter 1: Paul's Condition

1   Mark D. Nanos, *The Galatians Debate: Contemporary Issues in Rhetorical and Historical Interpretation* (Peabody, MA. Hendrickson, 2002), 29.
2   James D. G. Dunn, *Black's New Testament Commentary: The Epistle to the Galatians* (Peabody, MA: Hendrickson, 2006), 39.
3   Ibid., 47.
4   Gordon Fee, *Galatians: Pentecostal Commentary* (Dorset, United Kingdom: Deo Publishing, 2007), 248.
5   Dunn, *Black's New Testament Commentary,* 25.
6   Ibid., 167.
7   F. F. Bruce. *The Epistle to the Galatians: New International Greek Testament Commentary* (Grand Rapids, MI: Eerdmans, 1982), 2622, Kindle.
8   Frank E. Gaebelein, *The Expositor's Bible Commentary,* vol. 10 (Grand Rapids, MI. Zondervan Publishing, 1976), 411.
9   Stephen Andrew Cooper, *Marius Victorinus' Commentary on Galatians* (New York, NY: Oxford University Press, 2005), 92.
10 Gordon Fee, *God's Empowering Presence* (Peabody, MA: Hendrickson, 1994), 420.
11 Fee, *God's Empowering Presence,* 374.
12 W. E. Vine, *New Testament Word Pictures: Romans to Revelation* (Nashville, TN: Thomas Nelson, 2015), 75.
13 Merrill C. Tenney, *The Expositor's Bible Commentary,* vol. 9 (Grand Rapids, MI: Zondervan, 1981), 152.
14 Ibid., 151.
15 Ibid., 151.
16 James W. Goll, *Releasing Spiritual Gifts Today* (New Kensington, PA: Whitaker House, 2016), 770, Kindle.
17 Jerry Bridges, *The Fruitful Life: The Overflow of God's Love through You* (Colorado Springs, CO: NavPress, 2014), 12.
18 Donald Gee, *The Fruit of the Spirit: Pentecostal Classic,* rev. ed. (Springfield, MO: Gospel Publishing House, 2010), 51.
19 Joseph Thayer, "Peripateo," Bible Study Tools, accessed June 30, 2017, http://www.biblestudytools.com/lexicons/greek/nas/peripateo.html.
20 Douglas J. Moo, *Galatians: Baker Exegetical Commentary on the New Testament* (Grand Rapids, MI: Baker Academic, 2013), 9424. Kindle.

21   Richard N. Longenecker, *Galatians*, vol. 41 of *Word Biblical Commentary* (Columbia, SC: Word, 1990), 249.

22   John H. Walton and Craig S. Keener, *Cultural Backgrounds* (Grand Rapids, MI: Zondervan, 2016), 2053, Kindle.

Chapter 2: Love

23   Bruce, *Commentary on Galatians*, 4532, Kindle.

24   Longenecker, *Galatians*, 260.

25   Dallas Willard, "Getting Love Right," (paper presented at the American Association of Christian Counselors Conference, Nashville, TN, September 15, 2007), 99, Kindle.

26   Fee, *Galatians,* 218.

27   Gee, *The Fruit of the Spirit*, 226.

28   D. A. Carson, "God's Love and God's Wrath," Gospel Translations, last updated June 9, 2010, accessed July 29, 2017. http://gospeltranslations.org/wiki/God%27s_Love_and_God%27s_Wrath.

Chapter 3: Joy

29   Moo, *Galatians*, 9736, Kindle.

30   Gee, *The Fruit of the Spirit*, 302.

31   Fung, *The New International Commentary on the New Testament,* 264.

32   Dunn, *Black's New Testament Commentary*, 310.

33   James Montgomery Boice, *The Expositor's Bible Commentary*, vol. 10 (Grand Rapids, MI. Zondervan, 1976), 498.

34   Longenecker, *Galatians*, 261.

35   Alexander, Rosner, Carson, and Goldsworthy, *New Dictionary of Biblical Theology,* 610.

36   John B. Polhill, *The New American Commentary: Acts*, vol. 26 (Nashville, TN: Broadman and Holman, 1992), 227.

37   Ben Witherington III, *The Acts of the Apostles: A Socio-Rhetorical Commentary* (Grand Rapids, MI: Eerdmans, 1998), 499.

38   Alexander, Rosner, Carson, and Goldsworthy, *New Dictionary of Biblical Theology,* 610.

39   Ibid.

Chapter 4: Peace

40   Boice, *The Expositor's Bible Commentary,* 498.

41   Willard M. Swartley, *Covenant of Peace: The Missing Peace in New Testament Theology and Ethics* (Grand Rapids, MI: Eerdmans, 2006), 35.

42 Ceslas Spicq, *Theological Lexicon of the New Testament* (Peabody, MA: Hendrickson Publishers, 1994), 427.

43 Tenney, *The Expositor's Bible Commentary*, 148.

44 Walton and Keener, *Cultural Backgrounds*, 1842, Kindle.

45 Boice, *The Expositor's Bible Commentary*, 498.

46 Fee, *Galatians*, 220.

47 Ibid.

Chapter 5: Patience

48 Earle L. Wilson, Alex R. G. Deasley, Barry L. Callen, *Galatians, Philippians, and Colossians: A Commentary for Bible Students* (Indianapolis, IN: Wesleyan Publishing, 2007), 127.

49 Fung, *The New International Commentary on the New Testament*, 266.

50 Fee, *Galatians*, 221.

51 Fee, *God's Empowering Presence*, 449–50.

52 Walton and Keener, *Cultural Backgrounds*, 2192, Kindle.

53 Moo, *Galatians*, 1587, Kindle.

Chapter 6: Kindness

54 Fung, *The New International Commentary on the New Testament*, 267.

55 Bedford, *A Theological Commentary on the Bible: Galatians*, 176.

56 Bridges, *The Fruitful Life*, 117.

57 F. F. Bruce, *The New International Commentary on the New Testament: The Epistle to the Colossians, to Philemon, and to the Ephesians* (Grand Rapids, MI: Eerdmans, 1984), 368.

58 Bruce, *Commentary on Galatians*, 4564, Kindle.

59 Grant Osborne, *Romans* (Downers Grove, IL: InterVarsity Press, 2004), 61.

60 Ibid.

61 Walton and Keener, *Cultural Backgrounds*, 1184, Kindle.

Chapter 7: Goodness

62 Fung, *The New International Commentary on the New Testament*, 268.

63 Longenecker, *Galatians*, 262.

64 Bruce, *Commentary on Galatians*, 4570, Kindle.

65 Fee, *God's Empowering Presence*, 451.

66 Don Hooser, "The Fruit of the Spirit-Goodness: God's Character and Man's Potential," Beyond Today, posted April 3, 2009, accessed January 2, 2017. https://www.ucg.org/the-good-news/the-fruit-of-the-spirit-goodness-gods-character-and-mans-potential.

67   Udo Schnelle, *Apostle Paul: His Life and Theology* (Grand Rapids, MI: Baker Academic, 2003), 567.
68   Gee, *The Fruit of the Spirit*, 731.

Chapter 8: Faithfulness

69   Moo, *Galatians*, 9765, Kindle.
70   Fee, *Galatians*, 222.
71   Alexander, Rosner, Carson, and Goldsworthy, *New Dictionary of Biblical Theology,* 489.
72   Kimber, *Disciples of the Holy Spirit*, xxi.
73   Marian Hiller, "Philo of Alexandria," Internet Encyclopedia of Philosophy, accessed January 8, 2017. http://www.iep.utm.edu/philo/#SH11m.
74   Goll, *Releasing Spiritual Gifts Today*, 1651, Kindle.
75   Bruce, *Commentary on Galatians*, 254.

Chapter 9: Gentleness

76   Geoffrey W. Bromiley, *Theological Dictionary of the New Testament: Abridged in One Volume* (Grand Rapids, MI: Eerdmans, 1985), 930.
77   Alexander, Rosner, Carson, and Goldsworthy, *New Dictionary of Biblical Theology*, 507.
78   Walton and Keener, *Cultural Backgrounds*, 1564, Kindle.
79   Barclay M. Newman, *Matthew: A Handbook on the Gospel of Matthew* (New York NY: United Bible Society, 1988), 345.
80   Murray J. Harris, *The Expositor's Bible Commentary,* vol. 10 (Grand Rapids, MI: Zondervan, 1976), 380.
81   D. A. Carson, *Matthew: The Expositor's Bible Commentary* (Grand Rapids, MI: Zondervan, 2010), 10578, Kindle.

Chapter 10: Self-Control

82   J. D. Douglas et al., *New Bible Dictionary*, 3rd ed. (Downers Grove, IL: InterVarsity Press, 1996), 1031.
83   Dunn, *Black's New Testament Commentary*, 312.
84   Moo, *Galatians*, 9780, Kindle.
85   Fung, *The New International Commentary on the New Testament*, 270.
86   Horst Balz and Gerhard Schneider, *Dictionary of the New Testament* (Grand Rapids, MI: T&T Clark, 1990), 55.
87   Ibid.

88 R. Scott Sullender, *Ancient Sins Modern Addictions: A Fresh Look at the Seven Deadly Sins* (Eugene, OR: Wipf and Stock, 2013), 174.
89 Russell Moore, *Tempted and Tried: Tempted and the Triumph of Christ* (Wheaton, IL: Crossway, 2011), 166.
90 Ibid., 182.
91 David L. Allen, *The New American Commentary Volume 35, Hebrews* (Nashville, TN: B&H Publishing Group, 2010), 517.

Spirit-Led Character Development

92 Kim John Payne, *The Soul of Discipline: The Simplicity Parenting Approach to Warm, Firm, and Calm Guidance—From Toddlers to Teens* (New York, NY: Random House Publishing, 2015), 695, Kindle.
93 George Barna, *Transforming Children into Spiritual Champions* (Grand Rapids, MI: Baker Publishing Group, 2013), 37.

Chapter 11: Foundational Formation Process

94 Don Detrick, *Growing Disciples Organically* (Sisters OR: Deep River Books, 2013), 702, Kindle.

Chapter 12: Love and Emotional Stability

95 Judith K. Balswick and Jack O. Balswick, *Authentic Human Sexuality: An Integrated Christian Approach* (Downers Grove, IL: InterVarsity Press, 2008), 167, Kindle.
96 Gary D. Chapman, *Anger: Taming a Powerful Emotion* (Chicago, IL: Moody Publishers, 2015), 29, Kindle.
97 John D. Gottman and Daniel Goleman, *Raising an Emotionally Intelligent Child* (New York, NY: Simon & Schuster, 2011), 2.
98 William M. Struthers, *Wired for Intimacy: How Pornography Hijacks the Male Brain* (Downers Grove, IL: InterVarsity Press, 2009), 868, Kindle.
99 Struthers, *Wired for Intimacy*, 869, Kindle.
100 Daniel J. Siegel, *The Mindful Brain: Reflection and Attunement in the Cultivation of Well-Being* (New York, NY. W. W. Norton & Company, 2007), 214, Kindle.
101 Daniel Goleman, Richard Boyatzis, and Annie McKey, *Leadership: Unleashing the Power of Emotional Intelligence* (Boston, MA: Harvard Business Review Press, 2013), 599, Kindle.
102 Gottman and Goleman, *Raising an Emotionally Intelligent Child*, 83.

Chapter 13: Joy and a Positive Attitude

103 Paul David Tripp, *Dangerous Calling: Confronting the Unique Challenges of Pastoral Ministry* (Wheaton, IL: Crossway, 2012), 35, Kindle.

104 Tripp, *Dangerous Calling*, 38, Kindle.

105 Goleman, Boyatzis, and McKey, *Leadership: Unleashing the Power of Emotional Intelligence*, 309, Kindle.

106 Ibid., 309, Kindle.

107 Joseph Ciaccio, *Totally Positive Teaching: A Five-Stage Approach to Energizing Students and Teachers* (Alexandria, VA: ASCD, 2004), 296, Kindle.

108 Ciaccio, *Totally Positive Teaching*, 313, Kindle.

109 Ibid., 329, Kindle.

110 Reggie McNeal, *A Work of Heart: Understanding How God Shapes Spiritual Leaders* (San Francisco, CA: Jossey-Bass, 2011), 185, Kindle.

111 Ciaccio, *Totally Positive Teaching*, 355, Kindle.

112 Ibid., 381, Kindle.

113 Ibid., 425, Kindle.

114 Ibid., 442, Kindle.

115 Ibid., 450, Kindle.

116 Philip Chircop, "Enthusiasm: A-Mused," accessed June 24, 2017, http:// www. philipchircop.com/ post/ 35151648435/enthusiasm-reflect-on-this-short-story-and-then.

Chapter 14: Peace and a Positive Attitude

117 Brene Brown, *The Gifts of Imperfection: Let Go of Who You Think You're Supposed to Be and Embrace Who You Are* (Center City, MI: Hazelden, 2010), 88, Kindle.

118 Robert S. McGee, *The Search for Significance: Seeing Your True Worth through God's Eyes* (Nashville, TN: Thomas Nelson, 2003), 265, Kindle.

119 Gottman and Goleman, *Raising an Emotionally Intelligent Child*, 93.

120 Brown, *Gifts of Imperfection*, 26, Kindle.

121 Ibid., 40, Kindle.

122 Ibid., 38, Kindle.

123 Kent Sayre, *Unstoppable Confidence: How to Use the Power of NLP to Be More Dynamic and Successful* (New York, NY: McGraw-Hill, 2008), 64, Kindle.

124 Sayre, *Unstoppable Confidence*, 31–54, Kindle.

Chapter 15: Patience and Tough-Mindedness

125 James T. Bradford, *Lead So Others Can Follow: Twelve Practices and Principles for Ministry* (Springfield, MO: Salibris Resources, 2015), 966, Kindle.

126 Dan B. Allender, *Leading with a Limp: Taking Full Advantage of Your Most Powerful Weakness* (Colorado Springs, CO: WaterBrook Press, 2006), 3.

127 Chuck DeGroat, *Toughest People to Love: How to Understand, Lead, and Love the Difficult People in Your Life—Including Yourself* (Grand Rapids, MI: Eerdmans, 2014), 23, Kindle.

128 Lynne C. Lancaster and David Stillman, *The M-Factor: How the Millennial Generation is Rocking the Workplace* (New York, NY: HarperCollins, 2010), 8, Kindle.

129 Tim Clinton and Joshua Straub, *God Attachment: Why You Believe, Act, and Feel the Way You Do About God* (New York, NY: Howard Books, 2010), 41, Kindle. Original quote by Nietzsche was: "If we have our own why in life, we shall get along with almost any how. Man does not strive for pleasure; only the Englishman does." Friedrich Nietzsche, "Maxims and Arrows," in *Twilight of the Idols,* accessed January 16, 2018, http://www.inp.uw.edu.pl/mdsie/Political_Thought/twilight-of-the-idols-friedrich-neitzsche.pdf.

Chapter 16: Kindness and Empathy

130 Henry Cloud *How People Grow: What the Bible Reveals about Personal Growth* (Grand Rapids, MI: Zondervan, 2009), 92, Kindle.

131 Clinton and Straub, *God Attachment,* 124, Kindle.

132 Brenda Branson and Paul J. Silva, *Violence among Us: Ministry to Families in Crisis* (Valley Forge, PA: Judson Press, 2007), 1291, Kindle.

133 Simon Sinek, *Leaders Eat Last: Why Some Teams Pull Together and Others Don't* (New York, NY: Penguin Publishing Group, 2014), 731, Kindle.

134 Sinek, *Leaders Eat Last,* 845, Kindle.

135 Ibid., 897, Kindle.

136 Ibid., 1668, Kindle.

137 DeGroat, *Toughest People to Love,* 50, Kindle.

138 Sinek, *Leaders Eat Last,* 3645, Kindle.

Chapter 17: Goodness and Maturity

139 McNeal, *A Work of Heart,* 77, Kindle.

140 A. W. Tozer. *The Root of the Righteous* (Chicago, IL: Moody Press, 1986), 165.

141 Sharon D. Parks, *Big Questions, Worthy Dreams: Mentoring Young Adults in Their Search for Meaning, Purpose, and Faith* (New York, NY: Jossey-Bass, 2011), 240, Kindle.

142 Payne, *The Soul of Discipline,* 713–18, Kindle.

143 Ibid, Kindle.

144 Jeffrey Jensen Arnett, *Emerging Adulthood: The Winding Road from the Late Teens through the Twenties*, 2nd ed. (Oxford England, UK: Oxford University Press, 2014), 330, Kindle.

Chapter 18: Faithfulness and Team Orientation

145 Patrick M. Lencioni, *The Advantage: Why Organizational Health Trumps Everything Else in Business* (San Francisco, CA: Jossey-Bass, 2012), 27, Kindle.
146 Patrick M. Lencioni, *Overcoming the Five Dysfunctions of a Team: A Field Guide for Leaders, Managers, and Facilitators* (San Francisco, CA: Jossey-Bass, 2005), 14, Kindle.
147 Eddie Gibbs and Ryan K. Bolger, *Leadership Next: Changing Leaders in a Changing Culture* (Downers Grove, IL: InterVarsity Press, 2005), 1127, Kindle.
148 Max De Pree, *Leadership Is an Art* (New York, NY: Doubleday, 2004), 11, Kindle.
149 Ibid., 24, Kindle.
150 Ibid., 24, Kindle.
151 Edward H. Hammett, *Spiritual Leadership in a Secular Age: Building Bridges Instead of Barriers* (St. Louis, MO: Chalice Press, 2005), 210, Kindle.
152 Judith E. Glaser, *Creating We: Change I-Thinking to We-Thinking and Build a Healthy, Thriving Organization* (Avon, MA: Platinum Press, 2007), 5557, Kindle.

Chapter 19: Gentleness and Conscientiousness

153 Steve Ogne and Tim Roehl, *TransforMissional Coaching* (Nashville, TN: B&H Publishing, 2008), 205, Kindle.
154 Brent Roberts, "Conscientiousness: A Primer," accessed July 10, 2017. https://www.brookings.edu/research/conscientiousness-a-primer/.
155 Kara E. Powell and Chap Clark, *Sticky Faith: Everyday Ideas to Build Lasting Faith in Your Kids* (Grand Rapids, MI: Zondervan, 2011), 45, Kindle.
156 Adrain Furnham, *The Engaging Manager* (London, UK: Palgrave McMillan, 2012), 102, Kindle.
157 Paul Hammerness, "Staying Healthy: Raising Your Conscientiousness," accessed July 10, 2017, http://www.health.harvard.edu/staying-helathy/raising-your-conscientiousness.
158 Ibid.

Chapter 20: Self-Control and Disciplines

159 Cloud and Townsend, *How People Grow*, 247, Kindle.
160 Scott M. Peck, *The Road Less Traveled: A New Psychology of Love, Traditional Values and Spiritual Growth* (New York, NY: Touchstone, 2012), 19, Kindle.

161 Joshua Straub, *Safe House: How Emotional Safety is the Key to Raising Kids Who Live, Love, and Lead Well* (Colorado Springs, CO: The Crown Publishing Group, 2015), 112, Kindle.

162 Straub, *Safe House*, 112, Kindle.

163 Cloud and Townsend, *How People Grow*, 81, Kindle.

164 Payne, *The Soul of Discipline*, 319, Kindle.

165 Thom S. Rainer and Jess W. Rainer, *The Millennials: Connecting to America's Largest Generation* (Nashville, TN: Broadman & Holman, 2010), 4062, Kindle.

166 Paul David Tripp, *Age of Opportunity: A Biblical Guide to Parenting Teens* (Phillipsburg, PA: Presbyterian and Reformed Publishing, 2001), 116, Kindle.

167 Daniel J. Siegel and Tina Payne Bryson, *No-Drama Discipline: The Whole-Brain Way to Calm the Chaos and Nurture Your Child's Developing Mind* (New York, NY: Random House, Publishing Group. 2014), 2195, Kindle.

168 Branson and Silva, *Violence among Us*, 956, Kindle.

169 Stu Weber, *Tender Warrior* (New York, NY: Random House, 2009), 322, Kindle.

170 Ibid., 771, Kindle.

171 Ibid., 2086, Kindle.

Chapter 21: Character Development Curriculum

172 Mark D. Nanos, *The Galatians Debate: Contemporary Issues in Rhetorical and Historical Interpretation* (Peabody, MA: Hendrickson, 2002), 29.

173 James D. G. Dunn, *Black's New Testament Commentary: The Epistle to the Galatians* (Peabody, MA: Hendrickson, 2006), 47.

174 Frank E. Gaebelein, *The Expositor's Bible Commentary*, vol. 10 (Grand Rapids, MI. Zondervan Publishing, 1976), 411.

175 Scot McKnight, *Galatians: The NIV Application Commentary* (Grand Rapids, MI: Zondervan, 1995), 40.

176 Boa, Kenneth. *Conformed to His Image: Biblical and Practical Approaches to Spiritual Formation*. (Grand Rapids, MI: Zondervan Publishing), 3293, Kindle.

177 Andy Stanley, *Deep and Wide: Creating Churches Unchurched People Love to Attend* (Grand Rapids, MI: Zondervan, 2016), 137, Kindle.

178 Troy Jones, *Recalibrate Your Church: How Your Church Can Reach Its Full Kingdom Impact*, (Renton, WA: Recalibrate Group, 2016), 1928, Kindle.

179 Henry Cloud and John Townsend, *How People Grow: What the Bible Reveals About Personal Growth* (Grand Rapids, MI: Zondervan, 2009), 122, Kindle.

180 Don Detrick, *Growing Disciples Organically* (Sisters, OR: Deep River Books, 2013), 702, Kindle.

181 Gordon Fee, *God's Empowering Presence* (Peabody, MA: Hendrickson, 1994), 374, Kindle.

182 Merrill C. Tenney, *The Expositor's Bible Commentary*, vol. 9 (Grand Rapids, MI: Zondervan, 1981), 152.

183 Tenney, *The Expositor's Bible Commentary*, 151.

184 James W. Goll, *Releasing Spiritual Gifts Today* (New Kensington, PA: Whitaker House, 2016), 770, Kindle.

185 F. F. Bruce, *Commentary on Galatians*, New International Greek Testament Commentary (Grand Rapids, MI: Paternoster Press, 1992), 4532, Kindle.

186 Dallas Willard, "Getting Love Right," paper submitted at the American Association of Christian Counselors Conference, 2012), 99, Kindle.

187 Gary D. Chapman, *Anger: Taming a Powerful Emotion* (Chicago, IL: Moody Publishers, 2015), 29, Kindle.

188 John D. Gottman and Daniel Goleman, *Raising an Emotionally Intelligent Child* (New York, NY: Simon & Schuster, 2011), 2.

189 Daniel Goleman, Richard Boyatzis and Annie McKey, *Primal leadership: Unleashing the Power of Emotional Intelligence* (Boston, MA: Harvard Business Review Press, 2013), 599, Kindle.

190 Gottman and Goleman, *Raising an Emotionally Intelligent Child,* 83.

191 Douglas J. Moo, *Galatians: Baker Exegetical Commentary on the New Testament* (Grand Rapids, MI: Baker Academic Publishing, 2013), 9736, Kindle.

192 Ronald Y. K. Fung, *The New International Commentary on the New Testament: The Epistle to the Galatians* (Grand Rapids, MI: Eerdmans, 1988), 264.

193 James Montgomery Boice, *The Expositor's Bible Commentary*, vol. 10 (Grand Rapids, MI: Zondervan, 1976), 498.

194 Paul David Tripp, *Dangerous Calling: Confronting the Unique Challenges of Pastoral Ministry* (Wheaton, IL: Crossway, 2012), 35, Kindle.

195 Gottman and Goleman, *Raising an Emotionally Intelligent Child,* 309–28.

196 Joseph Ciaccio, *Totally Positive Teaching* (Alexandria, VA: ASCD, 2004), 442, Kindle.

197 Moo, *Galatians*, 9465, Kindle.

198 Fung, *The Epistle to the Galatians*, 265.

199 Fee, *Galatians*, 220.

200 Brene Brown, *The Gifts of Imperfection: Let Go of Who You Think You're Supposed to Be and Embrace Who You Are* (Center City, MI: Hazelden, 2010), 88, Kindle.

201 Robert S. McGee, *The Search for Significance: Seeing Your True Worth through God's Eyes* (Nashville, TN: Thomas Nelson, 2003), 265.

202 Gottman and Goleman, *Raising an Emotionally Intelligent Child,* 93.

203 Kent Sayre, *Unstoppable Confidence: How to Use the Power of NLP to Be More Dynamic and Successful* (New York, NY: McGraw-Hill, 2008), 64, Kindle.

204 Fung, *The Epistle to the Galatians*, 266.

205 Ibid., 266.

206 Fee, *Galatians*, 449–50.

207 Walton and Keener, *Cultural Backgrounds*, 2192, Kindle.

208 Bradford, *Lead so Others Can Follow*, 966, Kindle.

209 Jessica Lahey, *The Gift of Failure: How the Best Parents Learn to Let Go So Their Children Can Succeed* (New York, NY: HarperCollins, 2015), 24, Kindle.

210 Tim Clinton and Joshua Straub, *God Attachment: Why You Believe, Act, and Feel the Way You Do About God* (New York, NY: Howard Books, 2010), 41, Kindle.

211 Fung, *The Epistle to the Galatians*, 267.

212 Nancy Elizabeth Bedford, *A Theological Commentary on the Bible: Galatians* (Louisville, KY: Westminster John Knox Press, 2016), 176.

213 Bruce, *The Epistle to the Galatians*, 4564, Kindle.

214 Walton and Keener, *Cultural Backgrounds*, 1184, Kindle.

215 Cloud and Townsend, *How People Grow*, 92, Kindle.

216 Simon Sinek, *Leaders Eat Last: Why Some Teams Pull Together and Others Don't* (New York, NY: Penguin Publishing Group, 2014), 845, Kindle.

217 Sinek, *Leaders Eat Last*, 31, Kindle.

218 Fung, *The Epistle to the Galatians*, 268.

219 Bruce, *The Epistle to the Galatians*, 4570, Kindle.

220 Bradford, *Lead So Others Can Follow*, 300, Kindle.

221 McNeal, *A Work of Heart*, 77, Kindle.

222 Paul D. Meier, Frank B. Minirth, Frank B. Wichern, Donald E. Ratcliff. *Introduction to Psychology and Counseling: Christian Perspectives and Applications* (Grand Rapids, MI: Baker Books, 2005), 48–50.

223 Moo, *The Epistle to the Galatians*, 9765, Kindle.

224 Fee, *Galatians*, 222.

225 Alexander, Rosner, Carson, Goldsworthy, *New Dictionary of Biblical Theology*, 489.

226 Patrick M. Lencioni, *The Advantage: Why Organizational Health Trumps Everything Else in Business* (San Francisco, CA: Jossey-Bass, 2012), 27, Kindle.

227 Eddie Gibbs and Ryan K. Bolger, *LeadershipNext: Changing Leaders in a Changing Culture* (Downers Grove, IL: InterVarsity Press, 2005), 1127, Kindle.

228 De Pree, *Leadership is an Art*, 24, Kindle.

229 Edward H. Hammett, *Spiritual Leadership in a Secular Age: Building Bridges Instead of Barriers* (St. Louis, MO: Chalice Press, 2005), 210, Kindle.

230 Fung, *The Epistle to the Galatians*, 269.

231 Walton and Keener, *Cultural Backgrounds*, 1633, Kindle.

232 Murray J. Harris, *The Expositor's Bible Commentary*, vol. 10 (Grand Rapids, MI: Zondervan, 1976), 380.

233 Steve Ogne and Tim Roehl, *TransforMissional Coaching* (Nashville, TN: B&H Publishing Group, 2008), 205, Kindle.

234 Adrain Furnham, *The Engaging Manager* (London, UK: Palgrave McMillan, 2012), 102, Kindle.

235 Paul Hammerness, "Staying Healthy: Raising Your Conscientiousness" (accessed July 10, 2017) http://www.health.harvard.edu/staying-helathy/raising-your-conscientiousness.

236 Ibid.

237 Moo, *Galatians*, 9779, Kindle.

238 Dunn, *Black's New Testament Commentary*, 312.

239 Fung, *The Epistle to the Galatians*, 270, Kindle.

240 Cloud and Townsend, *How People Grow*, 247, Kindle.

241 Scott M. Peck, *The Road Less Traveled: A New Psychology of Love, Traditional Values and Spiritual Growth* (New York NY: Touchstone, 2012), 19, Kindle.

242 Kim John Payne, *The Soul of Discipline*, 319–24, Kindle.

ABOUT THE AUTHOR

Phil Rasmussen, DMin | VP church relations
Phil.Rasmussen@northwestu.edu

Phil Rasmussen and his wife, Brenda, celebrated thirty-five years of marriage in 2020. They have two married children and two grandchildren. Their son, Kramer, is married to Kylie, and they serve as youth pastors at Churchome (churchome.org) in Kirkland, Washington. Phil and Brenda's daughter, Kaitlyn, is married to Jared McKinney, and they serve as pastors at Canvas Church (Canvas. church/billings) in Billings, Montana. Phil served as youth and associate pastor at Shoreline Community Church in Seattle; district youth director for the Northwest Ministry Network; and assistant national youth director in Springfield, Missouri. He served at Northwest University as the campus pastor and is currently VP of church relations and spiritual formation. Phil is a certified life coach and has completed a doctor of ministry degree from the Assemblies of God Theological Seminary (AGTS) in counseling with an emphasis in leadership.

Brenda serves as a professor of music at Northwest University. Her primary focus is in music theory and worship leader development. She directs a 130-voice gospel and worship choir, which travels and ministers in churches and schools. Brenda has a music degree from Northwest University as well as an advanced degree in music pedagogy from the Royal Conservatory of Music at the University of Toronto.

Brenda Rasmussen | music professor
Brenda.Rasmussen@northwestu.edu